DK EYEWITNESS TRAVEL

DUBLIN

POLLY PHILLIMORE AND ANDREW SANGER

Penguin
Random
House

Top 10 Dublin Highlights

The Top 10 of Everything

CONTENTS

Dublin and Ireland Area by Area

Streetsmart

Within each Top 10 list in this book, no hierarchy of quality or popularity is implied. All 10 are, in the editor's opinion, of roughly equal merit.

Front cover and spine *Ha'penny Bridge, linking the Temple Bar area and Liffey Street, Dublin*
Back cover *Courtyard of Dublin Castle*
Title page *City Hall dome, Dublin*

The information in this DK Eyewitness Top 10 Travel Guide is checked regularly. Every effort has been made to ensure that this book is as up-to-date as possible at the time of going to press. Some details, however, such as telephone numbers, opening hours, prices, gallery hanging arrangements and travel information, are liable to change. The publishers cannot accept responsibility for any consequences arising from the use of this book, nor for any material on third party websites, and cannot guarantee that any website address in this book will be a suitable source of travel information. We value the views and suggestions of our readers very highly. Please write to: Publisher, DK Eyewitness Travel Guides, Dorling Kindersley, 80 Strand, London WC2R 0RL, Great Britain, or email travelguides@dk.com

Welcome to
Dublin

"The craic". For many people, these two words completely sum up the spirit of Dublin, and just like the city, they represent a bubbling, sparky mix of fun and banter, fellow-feeling, warmth and conviviality. This is quite possibly the most sociable city in the world – and with Eyewitness Top 10 Dublin, it's yours to explore.

Dublin is a place that loves to party, as any evening spent on the cobblestones of the hyperactive **Temple Bar** district will prove. But Ireland's capital has much more to offer than just its famous pubs. It boasts gorgeous **Georgian architecture** and a number of world-class **museums** and **galleries,** many of them free to visit, and some of them gathered around the picturesque quadrangles of ancient **Trinity College**. The city has had a fairly turbulent history, beginning with Celts and Vikings, and tied together by threads of mass migration and a titanic struggle for independence. Exciting interactive attractions such as **EPIC Ireland** and **GPO Witness History** will immerse you in all these stories. Dublin also has a major literary tradition, spanning Joyce and Yeats, Swift and Wilde, Samuel Beckett and Roddy Doyle – as well as a vibrant **live music** scene that will have you reeling and jigging all through your stay.

Beyond the metropolis, Ireland is a nation rich in myths and legends and enlivened by laughter, with irresistible coastal scenery all the way from **Kerry** to **Donegal**, as well as a burgeoning food culture in cities such as **Kilkenny** and **Cork**. Whether you're coming for a weekend or a week, Top 10 Dublin brings together the best that the city and country can offer, from atmospheric monastic ruins and fine art to a peerless pint of Guinness or plate of prawns or oysters. The guide gives you insider tips throughout, plus five easy-to-follow itineraries designed to help you visit a clutch of sights in a short space of time. Add inspiring photography and detailed maps, and you've got the essential pocket-sized travel companion. **Enjoy the craic, enjoy the book, and enjoy Dublin.**

Clockwise from top: **The headland at Howth, Titanic Belfast, the Famine Memorial in Dublin, Temple Bar pub, the Giant's Causeway, colourful buildings in Dublin Castle grounds, Bantry Bay**

Exploring Dublin

Dublin is a place to take your time over: linger over a pint, share a story, watch the River Liffey glide by. But if your time is limited, here's how to grab the city's highlights in a whistle-stop weekend, along with a fun and action-packed, week-long driving tour taking in the best of Ireland.

The **Guinness Storehouse** is the best place to learn all about Ireland's national drink.

Key
— Two-day itinerary
— Seven-day itinerary

Two Days in Dublin

Day ❶
MORNING
From College Green, wander through the courtyards of **Trinity College** *(see pp12–13)*, dropping into the Old Library to marvel at the Book of Kells. Next head for the **National Museum** *(see pp14–15)*, choosing between Viking skeletons in the Archaeology Museum and the Dead Zoo at the Natural History Museum. Stop for lunch at the museum's café.

AFTERNOON
Swerve into grassy **St Stephen's Green** *(see p61)* for a lakeside walk, then window-shop your way along Grafton Street en route to the **Temple Bar** cultural quarter *(see pp22–3)*, which buzzes with attractions. Project Arts Centre and the Irish Film Institute have entertainment options for later, or you can just hit the bars. If the madness gets too much, nearby **Christ Church Cathedral** offers a quiet spot for some contemplation *(see pp24–5)*.

Day ❷
MORNING
Start with a sobering circuit of **Kilmainham Gaol** *(see pp32–3)*: it pays to pre-book; the first tour is at 9:45am (or 9:15am Jul–Sep). Then stroll the tree-lined avenue to Kilmainham Hospital, for cutting-edge art at IMMA. Its basement café is great for lunch.

AFTERNOON
It's a shortish walk to the **Guinness Storehouse** *(see pp30–31)*, for a panoramic pint in the Gravity Bar before returning to downtown Dublin, perhaps via the **Brazen Head**,

Dublin's oldest pub *(see p51)*. If you've time, **Dublin Castle** has miles of wandering and a monumental free storehouse of manuscripts and decorative arts *(see pp18–19)*.

Seven Days in Ireland

Day ❶ and ❷
Follow the two-day Dublin itinerary.

Day ❸
WICKLOW MOUNTAINS
For a hit of wild hills, head south into County Wicklow, spending a morning at fountain-sprinkled **Powerscourt Estate** *(see p75)*, then on to striking **Glendalough** *(see p84)*, for enigmatic monastic ruins and a lovely walk by the lakeside. Overnight in **Kilkenny**, with its brace of Michelin-starred restaurants *(see p88)*.

Day ❹
CORK
Ireland's second city *(see p95)* has a truly continental air, with a lip-smacking food scene and top-class music and ballet at the **Opera House** *(see p96)*. For a less frenetic itinerary, skip Galway (see below) and add a day at nearby **Kinsale** *(see p96)*, treating yourself to super-fresh shellfish on the multicoloured seafront.

Day ❺
KILLARNEY
Forty square miles of lakes, mountains and marauding red deer await in **Killarney National Park** – the way to see it all is by taking a jaunt in a car, or a traditional pony-and-trap *(see p91)*. Nearby **Kenmare** *(see p92)* has good options for dinner and digs.

Day ❻
DINGLE PENINSULA
The Ring of Kerry has endless dramatic driving, and a loop around the Dingle Peninsula gives a great flavour, taking in ocean views, early Christian relics and lunch at **Dingle's Charthouse Restaurant** *(see p93)*.

Day ❼
GALWAY CITY
The cobbled city of **Galway** *(see p105)* is full of live music and bustling pubs – it even has its own Latin Quarter.

Cobh, County Cork, has one of the world's largest natural harbours.

Top 10 Dublin Highlights

The magnificent Long Room at
Trinity College's Old Library, Dublin

🔟 Dublin Highlights

One of the most visited capitals in Europe, Dublin is a city steeped in history. Huddled together within a compact area are Viking remains, medieval cathedrals and churches, Georgian squares and world-class museums. But it's not just about buildings and artifacts – music, theatre, literature and pubs play just as strong a part in Dublin's make-up and atmosphere.

Trinity College ①

The elder statesman of Ireland's universities, Trinity is also one of the oldest in Europe. Its buildings and grounds are a landmark in the heart of the city (see pp12–13).

② National Museum of Ireland

Ranging from dinosaurs to military history, three collections in three locations make up this outstanding museum (see pp14–15).

Greater Dublin

GLASNEVIN · MARINO · CABRA · Royal Canal · PHIBSBOROUGH · Phoenix Park · ⑩ · SMITHFIELD · Connolly Station · Liffey · ⑨ · ⑧ · DUBLIN · Area of main Dublin map · KILMAINHAM · BALLSBRIDGE · RANELAGH

0 km 2
0 miles 2

National Gallery of Ireland ③

Wonderful Italian, French, Dutch and Spanish works are exhibited here, alongside a great collection of Irish art (see pp16–17).

④ Dublin Castle

The castle was built into the city's medieval walls and protected by the River Liffey to the north and in the south and east by the now underground River Poddle (see pp18–21).

5 Temple Bar
This ancient part of the city has been revamped into one of its busiest areas. There is no shortage of places to eat and drink *(see pp22–3)*.

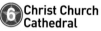

6 Christ Church Cathedral
Gothic, Romanesque and Victorian features jostle for attention in this former Viking church *(see pp24–5)*.

7 St Patrick's Cathedral
Known colloquially as the "People's Cathedral", this is one of the earliest Christian sites in the city and is the Protestant community's main place of worship in the capital *(see pp28–9)*.

8 Guinness Storehouse
A pint of Guinness could be the country's national symbol. This exhibition at the Guinness Brewery ends with a free pint of the black stuff *(see pp30–31)*.

9 Kilmainham Gaol and Hospital
After a sobering tour of the one-time prison, lighten the mood at the former hospital, which now houses the Irish Museum of Modern Art *(see pp32–3)*.

10 Phoenix Park
This is one of the largest city parks in Europe. Historic monuments and Dublin Zoo are only two of its delights *(see pp34–5)*.

⭐ Trinity College

Trinity College is Dublin's most famous educational institution and, since its foundation in the 16th century, has produced many impressive alumni, among them Jonathan Swift, William Congreve, Oliver Goldsmith, Oscar Wilde, Bram Stoker and Samuel Beckett. Entering through the college's West Front is like walking into a bucolic time-warp: a cobbled quadrangle, smooth green lawns and an array of fine 18th- and 19th-century buildings. A number of the buildings are open to the public, the most outstanding being the Old Library, home to one of the country's greatest treasures, the *Book of Kells*.

NEED TO KNOW

MAP F4 ■ College Green, Dublin 2

■ 01-896 1000

■ www.tcd.ie

Open Jun–Sep: 9:30am–5pm Mon–Sat, 9:30am–4:30pm Sun; Oct–May: 9:30am–5pm Mon–Sat, noon–4:30pm Sun (library)

Adm €9

■ In South Frederick Street a very good Italian delicatessen, Dunne & Crescenzi, serves delicious snacks and meals.

■ The exhibition "The Book of Kells: Turning Darkness into Light" explains the history and background to illuminated manuscripts and includes full-scale reproductions of the glorious *Book of Kells*.

1 Front Arch
College Green, facing the Front Arch entrance to Trinity, was originally called Hoggen Green. The statues of Edmund Burke and Oliver Goldsmith flanking the entrance are by sculptor John Foley.

2 Douglas Hyde Gallery
One of Ireland's leading contemporary art galleries, the Douglas Hyde has exhibitions by both emerging and well-established artists.

3 Chapel
The chapel is the only one in Ireland shared by all denominations. The stained-glass window above the altar dates from 1867.

4 Old Library
Entry to the Old Library (below), built between 1712 and 1732, is from Fellows' Square. The finest feature is the magnificent 64-m (200-ft) Long Room, with two tiers of antiquated oak bookcases holding more than 200,000 books.

5 Berkeley Library Building

In front of Paul Koralek's 1967 creation is the sculpture *Sphere within a Sphere* (1982) by Arnaldo Pomodoro **(above)**.

THE HISTORY OF TRINITY COLLEGE

Founded in 1592 by Queen Elizabeth I on the site of All Hallows Monastery, Trinity College's aim was to provide young Protestants with an alternative to European universities where they might fall under the influence of Catholicism. The Anglican bias lasted into the 1970s.

Trinity College quadrangle

6 Museum Building

This fine Venetian-style edifice was completed in 1857; a pair of giant Irish deer skeletons stand guard in the magnificent hall. There are no museums here today, but Trinity's intriguing zoological collection is open to the public in summer – find it in the Zoology Building, nearby.

10 Book of Kells

This beautifully decorated illuminated manuscript **(left)** is one of the city's most treasured possessions. It is thought to date from around AD 800 and is believed to be the work of monks from the island of Iona in Scotland. The book was eventually given to Trinity by the Bishop of Meath in 1654.

7 Dining Hall

This grand dining hall, where Trinity's many students eat, was originally built by Richard Cassels in 1742, but it has been considerably altered over the past 250 years. It has been restored after a fire in 1984.

Campanile 9

This 30-m (100-ft) bell tower **(right)**, built by Sir Charles Lanyon, the architect of Queen's University in Belfast, is the centrepiece of Trinity's main quad, enclosed by 18th- and 19th-century buildings.

8 Samuel Beckett Theatre

Opened in 1992, the Samuel Beckett Theatre showcases the work of the drama department and hosts prestigious Irish and international companies.

🔟 ⭐ National Museum of Ireland

There are three different parts to this outstanding museum. The Kildare Street branch offers archaeology and history, as far back as prehistoric Ireland's early culture. The Merrion Street branch comprises the Museum of Natural History. The third branch of the museum is the Decorative Arts and History, Collins Barracks. This branch is a very different experience, with the most up-to-date display techniques portraying the country's decorative arts and social, military, economic and political history.

1 Façade
The exterior of the museum in Kildare Street (above) is an example of Victorian Palladian style. The rotunda is modelled on the Pantheon in Rome.

3 Treasury
Part of a hoard found in County Limerick in 1808, the Ardagh Chalice (below) is probably the museum's most famous object. The mid-8th-century chalice is a beautiful example of the Irish Early Christian metalworker's craft. Another beauty from this collection is the Tara Brooch (Archaeology Museum, Kildare Street).

NEED TO KNOW

MAP F5, A3 ■ www.museum.ie

Archaeology Museum: Kildare Street, Dublin 2

Natural History Museum: Merrion Street, Dublin 2

Decorative Arts and History, Collins Barracks: Benburb Street, Dublin 7

Open 10am–5pm Tue–Sat, 2–5pm Sun
■ 01 677 7444

Dis. access ground floor only (Natural History Museum and Archaeology Museum); full access (Collins Barracks)

■ There's an excellent café at Collins Barracks.

2 The Easter Rising: Understanding 1916
This exhibition covers the period of unrest between 1913 and 1923, from the Dublin Lockout, through the Easter Rising to the end of the Civil War (Decorative Arts and History, Collins Barracks).

4 What's In Store
This wonderful exhibition is one of the highlights of the Decorative Arts and History, Collins Barracks branch of the museum. A visible storage display, it makes more than 16,000 objects (left) from the decorative arts collection accessible to the public in one space.

MUSEUM GUIDE

To visit all three parts of the city's National Museum on the same day, start with the Natural History Museum in Merrion Square. From here the Archaeology Museum is only a short walk: turn right at the lights on Baggot Street, head along the north side of St Stephen's Green, then turn right into Kildare Street. The easiest way to get from here to the third and last wing, Collins Barracks, is to take the handy tourist "Do Dublin" Hop-on Hop-off bus (www.do dublin.ie) over to the north side of the river.

5 Soldiers and Chiefs

This exhibition displays over 1,000 military artifacts, such as swords, uniforms, letters and firearms, as well as the fascinating Stokes Tapestry **(above)**, depicting scenes from army life and Irish history (Decorative Arts and History, Collins Barracks).

6 Irish Silver

The silver collection shows a huge variety of styles. The arrival of French Huguenot silversmiths in Dublin had a strong influence on local design (Decorative Arts and History, Collins Barracks).

7 Viking Collection

Ireland's Viking Age extended from AD 800 to 1150 and is evoked through objects found at a number of Viking graves and sites in and around Dublin (Archaeology Museum, Kildare Street).

8 Prehistoric Ireland

The Lurgan Longboat, dating from around 2500 BC, is made out of hollowed-out oak trunks 15 m (50 ft) long. Other pieces include the cast bronze horns, probably played like the Australian didgeridoo (Archaeology Museum, Kildare Street).

9 Ór – Ireland's Gold

This superb collection of ancient gold **(below)** was found in counties as far apart as County Clare and County Derry. The pieces show great skill and invention (Archaeology Museum, Kildare Street).

10 Fonthill Vase

This bluish-white vase is the only surviving example of porcelain to have left China in the 14th century and whose history can be traced from that moment on (Decorative Arts and History, Collins Barracks).

TOP 10 ⭐ National Gallery of Ireland

The National Gallery's outstanding collection of Western European art ranges from the Middle Ages to the mid-20th century and includes the most important gathering of Irish art in the world. The gallery was opened in January 1864. The Milltown Wing was added in 1903, the Beit Wing in 1968 and the Millennium Wing in 2002, the last bringing a huge improvement in exhibition space and public facilities. The gallery has benefited from some important donors during its history, including Countess Milltown, George Bernard Shaw, Sir Hugh Lane, Chester Beatty and Sir Alfred and Lady Beit. In mid-2017, the gallery completed a major renovation of its Dargan and Milltown wings.

1 The Liffey Swim
The gallery's Yeats Archive includes an impressive collection of Jack Butler Yeats' paintings, ranging from this early favourite, *The Liffey Swim* **(below)**, from 1923, to later expressionistic work such as *Grief* (1951).

2 The Taking of Christ
Caravaggio's moving 1602 work is the highlight of the gallery's display of Baroque paintings, which also takes in Orazio Gentileschi and Rutilio Manetti. Other Italian painters featured include Uccello, Titian, Tintoretto and Canaletto.

3 Amorino
The precocious Antonio Canova was the most gifted and innovative sculptor of the late 18th and early 19th centuries. This marble, *Amorino*, was commissioned in 1789 by John La Touche, who was the son of an Irish banker.

(5) Argenteuil Basin with a Single Sailboat

Claude Monet's 1874 painting **(above)** is a star in the gallery's very fine collection of 17th–19th-century French art.

(6) Kitchen Maid with the Supper at Emmaus

This early work by Diego Velázquez is part of a Spanish collection spanning five centuries. Other Spanish works include four canvases by Goya, including *Portrait of Doña Antonia Zárate*.

(7) The Cottage Girl

The ragged "cottage girl" **(below)** is one of Thomas Gainsborough's most famous "fancy pictures".

(4) Christ in the House of Martha and Mary

This painting **(above)** is interesting for being a collaborative work, painted in 1628 and featuring figures by Peter Paul Rubens in a landscape by Jan Brueghel the Younger.

(8) Still Life with a Mandolin

The strikingly vibrant *Still Life with a Mandolin* is from Pablo Picasso's time in Juan-les-Pins, on the Côte d'Azur, in 1924, where he worked on large-scale Cubist still-lifes, which are imbued with the exuberant light and colours of the sunny Mediterranean.

(9) Pastures at Malahide

This painting (1894–96) by Nathaniel Hone the Younger is part of a strong showing by Irish Impressionists. Hone travelled to Paris and the artists' colonies at Brittany and Barbizon.

(10) Self-Portrait as Timanthes

A fine collection of Irish art includes *Self-Portrait as Timanthes*, by 18th-century Neo-Classical painter James Barry, whose work influenced William Blake.

TOP10 ★ Dublin Castle

The imposing structure of Dublin Castle was a controversial symbol of British rule for 700 years, until it was formally handed over to Michael Collins and the Irish Free State in 1922. Commissioned by King John in the 13th century, the castle evolved from a medieval fortress into a vice-regal court and administrative centre. It has suffered numerous tribulations in its history, but the most concerted attack was in 1534, when it was besieged by "Silken Thomas" Fitzgerald (so called for his finely embroidered robes), who had renounced his allegiance to the English Crown. Its current use is primarily ceremonial. Visitors can tour the ornate state apartments and wander freely around the courtyards and museums.

BUILDING DUBLIN CASTLE

In 1204, 30 years after the Anglo-Norman landing in Ireland, King John ordered a castle to be built in Dublin. Much of this medieval castle was destroyed by fire in 1684 and Sir William Robinson completed the new apartments by 1688. Again, most of these were replaced in the 18th century.

① The Chester Beatty Library and Gallery

A stunning collection of artistic, religious and secular works from around the world dating from 2700 BC to the present (see pp20–21).

② Figure of Justice

Guarding the main entrance is the Figure of Justice. It faces the Upper Yard, turning its back on the city – as Dubliners cynically commented, an apt symbol of British justice.

③ Bermingham Tower Room

This former medieval prison was converted into a state apartment.

④ The Throne Room

This is the grandest state apartment in the castle. The throne (above) is flanked by roundels and ovals depicting Minerva, Jupiter, Juno and Mars.

⑤ The Bedford Tower

In 1907, the Irish "Crown Jewels" – a diamond St Patrick Star and Badge – were stolen from here and never recovered.

The imposing Dublin Castle

6 Gardens
To the back of the chapel are the Dubh Linn Gardens (above), located on the site of the "Black Pool" harbour from which the city gets its name.

7 The Chapel Royal
The exterior of this fine Gothic revival building is decorated with more than 100 heads, beautifully carved out of Tullamore limestone.

9 The Revenue Museum
In the crypt of the Chapel Royal, the exhibits here include a home-made still, used for distilling poitín, and examples of counterfeit goods.

8 St Patrick's Hall
Dedicated to Ireland's patron saint, the hall (right) has ceiling paintings by Valdre (1742–1814) depicting incidents in British and Irish history, such as St Patrick lighting the Pascal Fire on the Hill of Slane.

Plan of Dublin Castle

10 Viking Undercroft
Excavations show the remains of the original castle, including the moat and part of a 9th-century town.

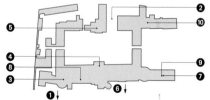

Chester Beatty Library Guide

Japanese picture book

1 Japanese Picture Books

Some of the finest pieces in the Japanese collection are the illustrated handscrolls and albums of a type known as *Nara Ehon* (Nara picture books).

2 Bust of Chester Beatty

A bust of Chester Beatty by the sculptor Carolyn Mulholland is on display in the atrium.

3 Mughal-era Indian Collection

This collection includes some of the best paintings and illustrated

A painting from the Mughal era

manuscripts produced under the guidance of the Mughal emperors Akbar, Shah Jahan and Jahangir.

4 Illuminated Manuscripts

Fine illuminated manuscripts can be found throughout the library, but the illustration of the Rose Garden of Sa'di, which was made for Baysunghur, a prince of the Timurid dynasty that ruled much of Iran in the 15th century, is one of the finest.

Japanese woodblock print

5 Woodblocks

The *ukiyo-e* woodblock prints complement the outstanding set of more than 700 prints known as *surimono*. These prints, like modern-day greetings cards, were created to mark special events or occasions.

6 Papyrus Texts

Papyrus is an aquatic plant from which ancient Egyptians made writing materials for their documents. One of the finest here is Paul's Letter to the Romans (around AD 180–200). The hieroglyphic and demotic papyri relate to administrative and burial practices.

7 Japanese Inrō

These tiny, intricately decorated boxes were used to store seals and medicines and are reproduced today by some perfumiers.

8 Chinese Collection

This eclectic display from the Qing dynasty includes snuff bottles, jade books and a stunning range of silk dragon robes.

9 The Qur'an Collection

This gathering of more than 260 Qur'ans and Qur'an fragments is considered to be the most important of its kind outside the Middle East. Ibn al-Bawwab is

Silk dragon robe, Chinese Collection

reputed to be one of the greatest medieval Islamic calligraphers and displayed here is the exquisite Qur'an he copied in Baghdad in 1001.

10 The Persian Poets

For connoisseurs of Persian poetry, famed Firdawsi, Nizami, Hafiz and Jami are just four of the authors that feature in the 330 manuscripts in this collection.

ALFRED CHESTER BEATTY

Alfred Chester Beatty was born in New York in 1875, and spent much of his childhood collecting stamps, minerals and Chinese snuff bottles. In adulthood, running a highly successful mining consultancy, he could afford to pursue his interests and gathered together this outstanding collection of Islamic manuscripts, Chinese, Japanese and other Asian Art. Beatty lived and worked in both New York and London before finally deciding to settle in Dublin in 1950. The first library for his collection was built on Shrewsbury Road, and was relocated to Dublin Castle in 2000. Beatty loved Ireland and contributed generously to its galleries and cultural institutions. In 1957 he became the country's first honorary citizen, and decided to leave his library in trust for the benefit of the public. He died in 1968 and was accorded a state funeral – the only private citizen ever to have received such an honour.

TOP 10 ARTIFACTS

1 Paul's Letter to the Romans c.AD 180–200 (Western collection)

2 Illuminated initial H, c.1153 *Walsingham Bible* (Western collection)

3 Egyptian love poems, 1160 BC (Western collection)

4 *Scenes from a Noh Play*, 17th century (East Asian collection)

5 *Qur'an*, copied by Ibn al-Bawwab, 1001 (Islamic collection)

6 *The Tale of Oriole*, late 17th century (East Asian collection)

7 Luke 6: 30-41, Four Gospels and the Acts of the Apostles, AD 200–250 (Western collection)

8 *The Madonna on a Grassy Bank*, Dürer, 1503 (Western collection)

9 Jade snuff bottle, c.1750–1800 (East Asian collection)

10 The Roleau Vase, early 18th century (East Asian collection)

(Displays change frequently; see website)

Rare, illuminated Western manuscripts

TOP 10 ⭐ **Temple Bar**

A lively enclave of cafés, bars and theatres, the Temple Bar area covers the cobbled streets that stretch between Dame Street and the River Liffey, and from Fishamble Street to Fleet Street. Known as Dublin's cultural quarter, Temple Bar always has something going on, especially in summer and autumn. Summer brings outdoor film screenings, street theatre and live music, while autumn sees the Dublin Theatre Festival, Culture Night and Fringe Festival.

1 City Hall
Built by Thomas Cooley in 1769–79, the building **(below)** was originally the Royal Exchange, but became the City Hall in the mid-19th century. Built of Portland stone, it is a fine example of Neo-Classical style *(see p63)*.

A lively pedestrianized cobbled street in Temple Bar

2 Merchant's Arch
A formal entry point to the area, the arch dates from the days when ships sailed right up the Liffey to dock and trade.

3 Meeting House Square
Named after a Quaker Meeting Hall, this is the centre of Temple Bar. It is the venue for concerts, plays **(below)** and the Saturday food market. Café tables, spilling out onto the street, all add to the atmosphere.

4 Irish Rock 'n' Roll Museum Experience
Set around gig venue the Button Factory and the iconic Temple Lane Studios, this interactive museum blasts through the history of Irish popular music.

5 Cow's Lane
This pedestrian street has designer boutiques and chic coffee bars. Fashion and gift stalls line the centre path at the Designer Mart every Saturday from spring to late autumn.

Plan of Temple Bar

⑦ Millennium Bridge

One of three pedestrian bridges that cross the Liffey, the Millennium Bridge's simple lines perfectly complement its more famous and more ornate companion, the Ha'penny Bridge *(see p64)*. The bridge links the shopping areas north and south of the Liffey.

⑧ Gallery of Photography

This contemporary space hosts exhibitions by Irish and international photographers. There are also photography courses and dark rooms to rent.

⑨ Irish Film Institute

Housing the offices of independent film organizations, a lively bar and restaurant, as well as three screens, the Irish Film Institute was one of the first major cultural projects in Temple Bar.

⑥ Project Arts Centre

This modern arts centre, which began in 1966 as a three-week festival, is renowned for avant-garde theatre, dance, music and film *(see p48)*.

⑩ The Ark

There's a magical mini-amphitheatre and lots of bright spaces for getting crafty at Europe's first custom-built children's cultural centre **(below)**. Irish and international artists have developed the fun programmes, including exhibitions and theatre workshops *(see p46)*.

TOP 10 ⭐ Christ Church Cathedral

The spectacularly imposing cathedral that we see today is largely a result of 19th-century restoration. Dublin's first church, made of wood, was founded here in 1030 by Sitric Silkenbeard, the first Christian king of the Dublin Norsemen. In 1172, however, Norman Richard de Clare, known as Strongbow, demolished the first church and commissioned his own stone version. During the Reformation, the cathedral passed to the Protestant Church and, along with St Patrick's Cathedral, it remains within the Church of Ireland.

1 Medieval Carvings

Decorating the columns at the entrance to the North Transept, these 12th-century carvings depict two human faces with griffons and musicians. The middle pillar of the nave is adorned with fine Gothic heads.

2 Crypt

The vast crypt, the city's oldest structure, is unusual in that it runs the entire length of the building. It houses the treasury exhibition and a mummified cat and rat.

3 Strongbow's Tomb

The tomb of the Norman conqueror of Ireland (below) is a 16th-century replica. The effigy is not thought to be Strongbow. However, it is possible that the fragment lying beside the tomb may be part of the original.

4 Great Nave

The 25-m- (80-ft-) high nave (above) raises the spirits with its fine early Gothic arches. On the north side, the 13th-century wall leans out by 50 cm (1.5 ft), a result of the collapse of the south wall in 1562.

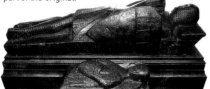

5 Romanesque Doorway

This doorway is a fine example of 12th-century Irish stonework. The carvings on the capitals depict a musical troupe.

STRONGBOW

In the 12th century, the exiled king of Leinster, Dermot MacMurrough, looked to the Anglo-Normans for help to recover his kingdom. Richard de Clare, also known as Strongbow, answered the call and arrived with his knights. He routed Leinster and conquered Dublin, then affirmed his loyalty to Henry II. It began centuries of English hold over Irish land.

6 Bridge to Synod Hall

This ornate Gothic bridge (above) was added during the rebuilding of the cathedral in the 1870s. Synod Hall is home to Dublinia, a re-creation of medieval Dublin (see p62).

7 Chapel of St Laud

This chapel is named after the 5th-century Normandy Bishop of Coutances. The chapel used to hold the preserved heart of Dublin's 12th-century patron saint, Laurence O' Toole. However, the heart was stolen in 2012 and has not been recovered.

8 Lady Chapel

One of the other chapels opening off the central choir area is used to celebrate the daily Eucharist and provides a more intimate setting than the nave of the cathedral when numbers are small.

9 Lord Mayor's Pew

Generally known as the Civic Pew, but historically belonging to the Lord Mayor, it is kept in the north aisle, but is moved to the front of the nave when required for ceremonial use. It is decorated with a carving of the city; there is also a rest for the civic mace.

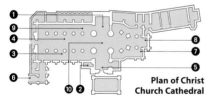

Plan of Christ Church Cathedral

10 Choir

At the centre of the church, the Victorian wooden stalls (above) are set out for the choir. The Archbishop's Throne is set in pride of place.

NEED TO KNOW

MAP D4

Christ Church Cathedral: Christchurch Place, Dublin 8; 01 677 8099; opening times vary, check website or call before visiting; closed 26 Dec; adm €6 (cathedral, crypt & treasury); partial dis. access; www.christchurchdublin.ie

Dublinia: Synod Hall; 01 679 4611; open Mar–Sep: 10am–6:30pm daily; Oct–Feb: 10:30am–5:30pm daily; last 1 hr before closing; adm €9.50, students and seniors €8.50, children €6 (combination tickets for Dublinia & cathedral available); www.dublinia.ie

■ Concerts are held in the main body of the cathedral and in the atmospheric crypt.

Following pages *Interior of St Patrick's Cathedral*

🔟 ⭐ St Patrick's Cathedral

St Patrick's, the Protestant Church of Ireland's national cathedral and commonly known as the "People's Cathedral", stands on an early Christian site where St Patrick is said to have baptized converts in a well in 450. Like Christ Church Cathedral, the original structure was made of wood and it was not until 1190, when Archbishop John Comyn founded St Patrick's, that it was rebuilt in stone and raised to the status of cathedral.

1 Nave
St Patrick's is the longest medieval church in Ireland and the nave **(below)**, with its carved pillars, reflects these immense proportions.

2 North Transept
Hanging above the arches of the North Transept are a number of flags commemorating Irish men and women who died in the service of the British Army.

3 South Transept
This former chapter house boasts a beautiful stained-glass window and numerous monuments. Particularly interesting is that of Archbishop Marsh which has fine carvings by Grinling Gibbons.

4 Choir
The choir **(above)** is adorned with swords, banners and helmets. These represent the different knights of St Patrick who, until 1869, underwent their services of investiture in this chapel. Another memorial honours Duke Frederick Schomberg, slain during fighting at the Battle of the Boyne.

5 Minot Tower
Believed to have been built for defence purposes, the almost 50-m (147-ft), 14th-century Minot Tower **(below)** still looks out of kilter with the rest of the cathedral.

7 Boyle Monument

The vast monument for the eminent Boyle family **(left)** is overrun with painted figures of the children of Richard Boyle, first Earl of Cork.

8 Graves of Jonathan Swift and Stella

One of the first ports of call for many visitors to the cathedral are the graves of the satirist Jonathan Swift *(see p42)* and his beloved Stella, positioned in the nave beneath brass tablets.

9 The Door of Reconciliation

A row between two 15th-century earls, Kildare and Ormond, reached stalemate when Ormond barricaded himself in the chapter house. Kildare cut a hole in the door and offered to shake hands. From this incident came the expression "chancing your arm". The door, with its hole, is on display in the North Transept.

JONATHAN SWIFT

Jonathan Swift was born in Dublin in 1667 and was educated at Trinity College *(see pp12–13)*. In 1694, he took holy orders and moved to England as tutor to young Esther Johnson at Moor Park in Surrey. Esther was to become the beloved "Stella" of his writings. Despite a reputation as a wit and pamphleteer, his ecclesiastical career was his primary concern and, in 1713, Swift was appointed dean of St Patrick's. On his death in 1745, he bequeathed £8,000 to build Dublin's St Patrick's Hospital.

10 South Aisle

Memorials here honour renowned Irish Protestants of the 20th century. Douglas Hyde, Ireland's first president and founder of the Gaelic League, is aptly remembered in Irish.

NEED TO KNOW

MAP D5 ■ St Patrick's Close, Dublin 2 ■ 01 453 9472 ■ www.stpatricks cathedral.ie

Open 9:30am–5pm Mon–Fri, 9am–5pm Sat, 9–10:30am & 12:30–2:30pm Sun (Mar–Oct: to 6pm Sat; 4:30–6pm Sun)

Adm €6.50, students and seniors €5.50, family €16

■ Choral evensong: 5:30pm Mon–Fri, 3:15pm Sun; Sung Eucharist: 11:15am Sun.

■ Services at Christmas and Easter are busy; try to arrive early.

6 Lady Chapel

At the east end of the church, this 13th-century building **(above)** was given over to the French Huguenots who arrived as refugees in the mid-17th century. They were allowed to worship here by the Dean and Chapter, and did so for almost 150 years.

🔟 ⭐ Guinness Storehouse

Ask the majority of people what they most associate with Ireland, and the likely answer will be Guinness. Together with whiskey, it is the national drink, famous for its malty flavour and smooth, creamy head. Arthur Guinness founded this immensely successful brewery in 1759; 250 years on, Guinness is the largest brewery in Europe and the beer is available in more than 150 countries worldwide. The excellent exhibition at St James's Gate covers all aspects of the production, and ends with a welcome free pint.

② Brewing Process

It takes a full 10 days to brew the perfect pint of Guinness. The roaster, kieve kettle and maturation vessel are brought to life using 3D-animated graphics.

③ History of Cooperage

Displays in this section (above) explain how expert coopers crafted the stout wooden barrels in times past. Metal casks have been used since the 1940s.

① Ingredients

The brewery tour begins with a dramatic introduction to each component of the black stuff: a massive barley pit, gleaming glass columns full of hops and yeast, and even a tumbling waterfall to represent the most fundamental ingredient of all – water (above).

NEED TO KNOW

MAP A5 ▪ St James's Gate, Dublin 8 ▪ 01 408 4800 ▪ www.guinness-storehouse.com

Open 9:30am–5pm daily; Jul & Aug: 9am–6pm.

Adm €20, students €18, children €13.50

▪ The Brewer's Dining Hall features an open kitchen and serves quiche, pies and signature beef and Guinness stew.

▪ Hold on to the perspex drop of Guinness given to you at the start – it is your ticket and enables you to claim your free pint.

▪ The area around the Guinness Storehouse is a bit isolated; the "Do Dublin" Hop-on Hop-off bus is a good way to get there.

4 Arthur Guinness Gallery

An 18th-century doctor, footman and bartender recount the fascinating life and times of Arthur Guinness. He founded his brewery in 1759 thanks to a bequest from his godfather – a Church of Ireland archbishop.

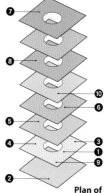

Plan of Guinness Storehouse

Key to Floorplan
- Seventh floor
- Sixth floor
- Fifth floor
- Fourth floor
- Third floor
- Second floor
- First floor
- Ground floor

ARTHUR GUINNESS

Arthur Guinness (1725–1803) first bought a lease on a brewery in Leixlip, near Dublin, in 1756. Three years later, he gave this to his brother when he signed the lease for St James's Gate. He married Olivia Whitmore in 1761, and ten of their 21 children lived to establish a dynasty that has now expanded into many activities worldwide.

5 Tasting Rooms

This multi-sensory zone brings the distinctive flavours to life; bartenders demonstrate how to enjoy your drop – sup the black stuff, not the creamy head.

7 Gravity Bar

Here's what most visitors have been waiting for – their free pint at the Gravity Bar, with its 360° views.

8 Guinness and Food

There are three separate dining options here, all with Guinness looming large on the menu.

9 Transport

This gallery **(above)** explores how Guinness has travelled the globe, and how it varies from nation to nation. It's now brewed in almost 50 countries – to the tune of 10 million glasses a day.

10 Guinness Academy

Learn how to pour the perfect pint here. The six-step ritual is as legendary as the beer itself – from the 119.5 seconds it takes to pour to the eventual settle.

Share Your Instagram Photos Using #StorehouseStory

6 Advertising

Immerse yourself in almost a century of ground-breaking campaigns **(above)**, featuring film and TV ads, and an interactive iPad area.

TOP 10 ⭐ Kilmainham Gaol and Hospital

Despite sharing the same name, these two sights could not be more different, both in their appearance and history. The forbidding gaol was built in 1796, its damp and grim conditions adversely affecting the health of the inmates. The jail closed in 1924 and wasn't touched again until it was restored as a museum in the 1960s. Kilmainham Hospital, built in the 1680s, was modelled on Les Invalides in Paris. It is now home to the Irish Museum of Modern Art (IMMA).

1 Exhibition
Housed in a modern hall of the gaol, this exhibition **(above)** puts visitors in the rather gruesome mood for what follows. On the ground floor is a section on hanging techniques, while upstairs deals with the bitter struggle for independence *(see p39)*.

2 Gaol Chapel
The most poignant story related about the chapel is the wedding here of Joseph Plunkett and Grace Gifford. They married on the eve of Plunkett's execution, and were allowed 10 minutes alone together before Plunkett was taken out and shot.

3 West Wing
It doesn't take much to imagine the horror of internment here **(left)**. The guide tells of the conditions that the prisoners were subjected to – hard labour and only 1 hour of candlelight a night.

4 Tour
A tour covering Irish history from 1796 to 1924 takes in the Stone Breaker's Yard, in which the leaders of the 1916 uprising were executed by firing squad *(see p39)*.

5 East Wing
A fine example of the "Panoptical" layout **(above)**, which is found in many Victorian prisons. The idea was to maximize light but allow for the constant surveillance of the prisoners.

6 Kilmainham Gate
This rather austere doorway is flanked by iron gates and sets the mood for a visit to the gaol. A tree-lined avenue links the fine surroundings of the Kilmainham Hospital to its much bleaker neighbour.

7 Gardens and Courtyard

The hospital's splendid and beautifully kept formal gardens were designed between 1710 and 1720 and laid out in the French style with herbs and medicinal plants. They have been restored to their former glory in recent years.

8 Hospital Chapel

The magnificent Baroque ceiling with its cherub heads and vegetable swags, was unlike anything seen in Ireland at that time. James Tabary, a Huguenot settler, carved the altar, reredos and rails from Irish oak in 1686.

THE HISTORY OF KILMAINHAM HOSPITAL

Kilmainham's Royal Hospital was built between 1680 and 1684 to the designs of Sir William Robinson, and is considered the most important 17th-century building in Ireland. Built for retired veterans, the hospital was handed over to the Free State in 1922 and served as the Garda headquarters in 1930–1950. It was one of the first buildings to benefit from Dublin's restoration programme in the 1980s. Beautifully renovated, it reopened in 1991 as the IMMA.

9 Great Hall

Formerly the soldiers' dining room, the Great Hall is very grand. The portraits of monarchs and viceroys, commissioned between 1690 and 1734, are the earliest surviving collection of institutional portraits in Ireland.

NEED TO KNOW

MAP A4

Kilmainham Gaol: Inchicore Rd, Dublin 8; 01 453 5984; open Jul–early Sep: 9am–6:45pm daily; early Sep–Jun: 9:30am–5:30pm daily; adm €9, seniors €7, children and students €5

Kilmainham Hospital & IMMA: Royal Hospital, Military Rd, Dublin 8; 01 612 9900; open 11:30am–5:30pm Tue–Fri, 10am–5:30pm Sat, noon–5:30pm Sun; www.imma.ie

- Some rooms of the hospital can be visited by guided tour only.

- There's an excellent café in the basement of the IMMA.

- The hospital grounds are vast, with lovely views, and ideal for a picnic.

10 IMMA

Since its move here in 1991, the Irish Museum of Modern Art (IMMA) **(above)** has made full use of the space available. There is a regularly changing resident collection of some 3,500 artworks, and innovative contemporary art features in touring exhibitions.

★ Phoenix Park

Surprisingly for such a small city, Phoenix Park is the largest enclosed urban park in Europe, covering an area of more than 1,750 acres (7 sq km). The name has no connection with the mythical bird but originates from the Gaelic *Fionn Uisce* which means "clear water" and refers to a spring that once existed here. Following the landscaping traditions of English parkland, complete with hundreds of deer, this is an idyllic place to escape from the bustling city centre. At the weekends whole families spend the day here, indulging in a variety of activities from dog-walking to jogging, golf practice, hurling matches, cricket and polo.

1 Deerfield
This 18th-century house, in the centre of the park **(below)**, was once the home of the British Chief Secretary for Ireland, Lord Cavendish, who was murdered in 1882 by an Irish nationalist. It is now the residence of the American ambassador.

2 Ashtown Castle
A visit to this tower house is included in the ticket to the Visitor Centre. It was once owned by the family of John Connell, who was an ancestor of Daniel O'Connell *(see p39)*. The tower was found inside the walls of the 18th-century Ashtown Lodge when the lodge was due to be demolished.

3 Magazine Fort
This fort became an arms depot after independence, but has been abandoned since the IRA raid in 1939, when more than one million rounds of ammunition were stolen.

4 Visitor Centre
The display here shows the changing face of the park, from 3500 BC to the present day. It also features a reconstruction of the Knockmaree Cist grave, which was found in the park in 1838. On Saturday, free tours depart from here to Áras an Uachtaráin.

5 Áras an Uachtaráin
This fine Palladian house **(above)** (1751), designed by Nathaniel Clements, was the Viceregal lodge. In 1938 it became the official home of the Irish president.

6 Phoenix Monument
The fourth Earl of Chesterfield erected this column **(left)** in 1747, topped with what is meant to be a phoenix, but looks more like an eagle than the mythical bird.

Map of Phoenix Park

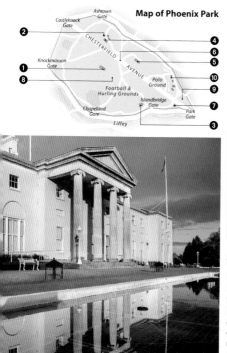

THE DEVELOPMENT OF PHOENIX PARK

In the 16th century, before the Reformation, the land at Phoenix Park belonged to the Knights Hospitallers of St John of Jerusalem. When the Dissolution of the Monasteries demanded the confiscation of all church lands, it became the property of the crown and the Duke of Ormond decided to enclose the land to provide a deer park for Charles II. The park was formalized and opened to the public in 1747.

9 People's Garden

Close to Park Gate, this is the only formal area of the whole park. Decimus Burton landscaped the area in the 1830s and the effect is gentle and restful, as the land-scaped flowerbeds merge with the wilder hillocks and ponds.

7 Wellington Testimonial

Designed by Robert Smirke in 1817, the monument celebrates the victories of the Duke of Wellington, and is the tallest obelisk in Europe at over 62 m (200 ft).

8 Papal Cross

The simplicity of the 35-m (116-ft) high stainless steel Papal Cross is part of its beauty. It was erected on the spot where Pope John Paul II celebrated Mass in 1979.

10 Dublin Zoo

Dublin Zoo (above) dates back to 1831 – the second oldest in Europe. The Kaziranga Forest Trail is modelled on a region in India. It is home to a growing herd of Indian elephants.

NEED TO KNOW

MAP T2

Phoenix Park: Park Gate, Conyngham Rd, Dublin 8; www.phoenixpark.ie

Visitor Centre: 01 677 0095; open Apr–Dec: 10am–6pm daily; Jan–Mar: 9.30am–5.30pm Wed–Sun; partial dis. access

Zoo: 01 474 8900; open Mar–Sep: 9:30am–6pm daily; Oct–Feb: 9:30am–dusk daily, last adm 1 hour before closing; adm €16.50, under-16s €11.80; www.dublinzoo.ie

■ Heuston is the closest station to Phoenix Park.

■ For great food and drink, head for Ryans pub *(see p50)*, just by the southeast gate in Parkgate Street.

■ Phoenix Park is not considered safe after dark.

Top 10 of Everything

The elegant cocktail bar at Pichet

Moments in History

Newgrange megalithic tomb

1 Newgrange
The first settlers arrived in Ireland from the Continent around 7000 BC, bringing with them farming skills and rudimentary tools. The megalithic stone tomb of the Stone Age at Newgrange *(see p76)* is thought to date from around 3200 BC and is one of the most important passage graves in Europe.

2 Celts Arrive
The Celts began to arrive in Ireland from Central Europe in around 500 BC. With their ability to produce iron weapons and implements, the Celts soon imposed their culture and language.

3 Christianity Comes to Ireland
Although the Romans never settled in Ireland it was through them that Christianity reached Irish shores. The first bishop was appointed in 431 but it is St Patrick *(see p40)* who is credited with the conversion of the pagan Celts and the establishment of the Church between 432 and 461.

St Patrick converting the Irish

4 Viking Ireland
The Vikings arrived in Ireland in AD 800 and established communities. In 1030 a wooden church was built where Christ Church Cathedral now stands *(see pp24–5)*.

5 First Irish Parliament
By the 1350s the Normans had settled in Ireland and introduced the feudal system of government, led by a justiciar who was head of the army, chief judge and top administrator. He was helped in his work by a council of officials, and would occasionally summon a parliament consisting of his council, bishops, abbots and feudal lords. By the end of the 14th century, representatives of counties and towns were part of the process known as the Lower House, or Commons.

The Battle of the Boyne

6 Battle of the Boyne
After his defeat by William of Orange at the Battle of the Boyne in 1690, James II fled to France leaving Ireland in the hands of the Protestant Ascendancy. These were English descendants of Tudor and Stuart settlers. The native Irish suffered for more than a century from the penal measures inflicted on them.

7 Georgian High Culture
Many of the most important sights in the city, such as Custom House *(see p44)*, were built in the Georgian era. Artists and musicians visited Dublin from all over Europe;

one of the highlights was the premiere of Handel's oratorio, *The Messiah*, in Dublin in 1741.

8 The Great Famine
The potato famine dominated 19th-century Ireland. The crop failed first in 1845 as a result of potato blight. As a result, about two million people died of starvation or emigrated, many to America, in a period that lasted until 1852.

Irish emigrants bound for America

9 The Easter Rising
On Easter Monday 1916, Patrick Pearse and others opposed to British rule proclaimed the Declaration of Independence from the General Post Office *(see p68)*. An uprising ensued. In December 1921 the Anglo-Irish treaty was signed, creating the Irish Free State.

10 Queen's Visit
Controversial with Irish republican groups, the Queen's state visit in 2011 was the first by a British monarch since Irish independence. It symbolized the thawing of relations between the two nations.

The Queen's state visit in 2011

TOP 10 POLITICIANS

Former Irish president, Mary Robinson

1 Henry Grattan
Grattan (1746–1820) entered Parliament in 1775 and was a great champion of the Catholic cause.

2 Theobald Wolfe Tone
Theobald Wolfe Tone (1763–98) was an Irish Republican and rebel who sought to overthrow English rule.

3 Daniel O'Connell
The greatest leader of Catholic Ireland, O'Connell (1775–1847) was a constant agitator against the Union.

4 Charles Stewart Parnell
Leader of the Irish Parliamentary Party in 1880, Parnell (1846–91) secured Gladstone's conversion to Home Rule.

5 Arthur Griffith
Arthur Griffith (1872–1922) launched Sinn Fein in 1906 and was elected president of the Dáil in 1922.

6 Patrick Pearse
Pearse (1879–1916) was executed for delivering the Irish Proclamation of Independence in 1916.

7 Michael Collins
Commander-in-Chief of the government forces in the Civil War, Michael Collins (1890–1922) was shot dead in his native County Cork.

8 Eamon de Valera
De Valera (1882–1975) was President of the Irish Republic from 1959 to 1973. His ideal was a 32-county Gaelic republic.

9 Charles Haughey
Prime minister for various terms from 1979 to 1992, Haughey (1925–2006) remains a controversial figure.

10 Mary Robinson
Barrister Mary Robinson was elected the first woman president of Ireland in 1990. She was in office until 1997.

🔟 Irish Legends and Myths

1 St Patrick

A 5th-century Roman Briton, Patrick was captured by Irish raiders and taken into slavery in Ulster. Escaping back to Britain, he became a priest and returned to Ireland to help convert the Irish. Extraordinary tales about him abound – he cured the sick, raised the dead, and rid Ireland of snakes by ringing his bell (see p38).

St Patrick

2 Punishment of the Children of Tuireann

For murdering his father, the sun god Lugh demanded that the three sons of Tuireann give him magical objects and perform difficult feats. Their last task was to make three shouts from the Hill of Miochaoin.

3 Cúchulainn

The boy Setanta had miraculous strength and loved the game of hurling. Invited to a feast by the legendary blacksmith Culain, Setanta arrived late and was met by the smith's ferocious guard dog. He killed the hound with his hurley stick and offered himself as a guard instead. He was renamed Cúchulainn, "hound of Culain".

4 The Children of Lir

The greatest of the *Tuatha dé Danann*, or fairy folk, was the sea god Lir. His four beloved children were turned into swans by their jealous stepmother Aoife, who condemned them to live forever in the waters off the coast of Ulster. Around 900 years later, a Christian named Caomhog broke the spell, and baptized them as they died.

5 Deirdre and the Exile of the Sons of Usnach

King Conchubar loved Deirdre, his harpist's beautiful daughter. The druid Cathbad foretold she would bring disaster, so her father kept her in solitude. But Deirdre loved Naoise, son of Usnach, who, with his brothers, took her to Scotland. After persuading them to return, Conchubar killed Usnach's sons. Deirdre, utterly grief-stricken, killed herself.

6 Cattle Raid of Cooley

Connacht's Queen Medb (Maeve) raided Ulster to seize the chief Daire's famous bull. All the men of Ulster being under a spell, Cúchulainn fought alone, killing all Medb's warriors. Medb retreated.

7 Destruction of Dinn Ríg

Cobthach of Bregia killed his brother Lóegaire, the King of Leinster. Some legends say that Lóegaire's grandson, Moen, was spared, but was made to drink of his grandfather's blood and was struck dumb. Later, Moen recovered

Children of Lir sculpture

his speech and was renamed Labraid ("speaks"). He eventually killed Cobthach by locking him in a house and burning him to death.

8 Oisin in Tír na nÓg
Fionn mac Cumhaill's son Oisin and Niamh, daughter of sea god Manannan, went to Tír na nÓg, paradise of eternal youth. After 300 years, homesick Oisin borrowed Niamh's magic horse to visit Ireland. His feet were not to touch the ground, but he fell from the horse, instantly aged 300 years and died.

Oisin and Niamh in Tír na nÓg

9 Pursuit of Diarmaid and Grainne
Fionn mac Cumhaill asked King Cormac for the hand of his daughter Grainne, but she eloped with Fionn's nephew Diarmaid. For a year and a day Diarmaid and Grainne fled, with the enraged Fionn in pursuit.

10 Salmon of Knowledge
The first person to taste the Salmon of Knowledge would gain prophetic powers. When Fionn mac Cumhaill visited Finnegas, the druid caught the fish. While it cooked, Fionn's thumb touched the salmon. Putting the thumb to his lips, he tasted the fish before Finnegas.

TOP 10 CELTIC TRADITIONS

Celtic Crosses at Clonmacnoise

1 Celtic Crosses
High, richly carved stone crucifixes with a central circle are a feature of Celtic churches and monasteries.

2 Celtic Design
Distinctive traditional interlocking patterns and symbols that decorate ancient Celtic jewellery have always remained popular in Ireland.

3 Language
The Irish language, also known as Gaelic, is spoken by about 1.7 million people today, and comes directly from the ancient Celtic inhabitants.

4 Céilí
A large social get-together where people drink, sing, dance and stamp their feet to traditional Irish folk music.

5 Hurling
This robust Celtic game requires hurleys (ash sticks), a *sliotar* (a leather ball) and a large dose of energy.

6 Musical Instruments
Uillean pipes, *bodhráns* (drums), tin whistles and other Celtic instruments remain at the heart of Irish folk music.

7 St Brigid's Crosses
Country people still weave rushes into these crosses and hang them up to protect their home against evil spirits.

8 Fairy Trees
An isolated tree in a field is generally not cut down because it is often considered bad luck.

9 Water Worship
Sacred springs, fairy wells and holy water still play a large part in many Irish people's religious beliefs.

10 Craic
The witty, relaxed conviviality, gossip and talk that makes life worth living.

TOP10 Dublin Writers

Writer James Joyce in 1904

1 James Joyce

The writer who most prolifically put Dublin on the literary map, Joyce (1882–1941) was born and educated in the city. He met Nora Barnacle on 16 June 1904 and, although they did not marry for 30 years, it became the date for events in his epic work *Ulysses*, published in Paris in 1922. *Dubliners* (1914), *Portrait of the Artist as a Young Man* (1916) and *Finnegans Wake* (1939) are among his other works.

2 George Bernard Shaw

Born in Dublin, Shaw (1856–1950) moved to England in 1876. Starting as a book reviewer for the *Pall Mall Gazette*, he was to become a prolific playwright; *The Devil's Disciple* (1897) and *Pygmalion* (1912) are just two of his works. He received the Nobel Prize for Literature in 1925.

3 William Butler Yeats

William Butler Yeats (1865–1939), brother of the painter Jack B Yeats, was born in Dublin. His first volume of poetry, *The Wanderings of Oisin and*

William Butler Yeats

Other Poems, was well received and later volumes confirmed his status as a leading poet. His play *On Baile's Strand* was chosen for the Abbey Theatre's opening in 1904 (see p70).

4 Jonathan Swift

Swift (1667–1745) was born and educated in Dublin (see p29) and established a reputation as a wit through his satirical works. *A Modest Proposal* (1729), one of his most brilliant – if grim – satires, suggested feeding poor children to the rich. It is ironic that his work *Gulliver's Travels* (1726) is a children's classic.

5 Oscar Wilde

Wilde (1854–1900) was born at Westland Row, Dublin, and became a classics scholar at Trinity College (see pp12–13) and later at Oxford. His highly popular plays, full of acid wit, include *An Ideal Husband* (1895) and *The Importance of Being Earnest* (1895). His imprisonment for homosexual offences inspired *The Ballad of Reading Gaol* (1898), but he died, destitute in Paris, in 1900.

Oscar Wilde sculpture in Merrion Square

6 Sean O'Casey

Dublin-born Sean O'Casey (1880–1964) worked on the railways and became an active trade unionist. He achieved instant success with *The Shadow of a Gunman* (1923), which was set in the Dublin slums, followed by the play *Juno and the Paycock* in 1924 and his best-known work, *The Plough and the Stars,* in 1926.

Irish novelist Elizabeth Bowen

7 Elizabeth Bowen
Although born in Dublin, Elizabeth Bowen (1899–1973) spent much of her childhood in Cork. Her years in wartime London are vividly evoked in her novels, including *The Heat of the Day* (1949).

8 Samuel Beckett
French Huguenot by descent, after a distinguished career at Trinity College, Beckett (1906–89) spent much of his life in France. The play *Waiting for Godot* (1952) made him an international name. He received the Nobel Prize for Literature in 1969.

9 John McGahern
Celebrated for his honest exploration of rural life in Ireland, McGahern (1934–2006) left the country after his early novel, *The Dark* (1965), was banned. He returned to country life in 1970 and lived on a farm until he died.

10 Patrick Kavanagh
Kavanagh (1904–67), born in Monaghan, went to London in 1939 and began a career as a journalist, poet and novelist. His reputation was established with a long and bitter poem on the hardships of rural life, *The Great Hunger* (1942).

TOP 10 IRISH WRITERS

1 Seamus Heaney
Ireland's most prominent poet, Heaney (1939–2013) won the Nobel Prize for Literature in 1995. *North* (1975) explores the Troubles in Northern Ireland.

2 William Trevor
William Trevor (1928–2016) was a master of the short story genre.

3 John Banville
A screenwriter, Banville (b.1945) is also a multi-award-winning novelist.

4 Anne Enright
Anne Enright (b. 1962) wrote the powerful novel *The Gathering* (2007), which won the prestigious Man Booker Prize.

5 Brian Friel
The successes of playwright Friel (b.1929) include *Dancing at Lughnasa* (1990).

6 Roddy Doyle
Renowned for his *Barrytown Trilogy* about Dublin life, Roddy Doyle (b.1958) won the Man Booker Prize in 1993 for *Paddy Clarke Ha Ha Ha*.

7 Edna O'Brien
The Country Girls (1960) was the first novel by award-winning poet and novelist O'Brien (b.1930).

8 Colm Tóibín
Tóibín (b.1955) was shortlisted for the 2000 Man Booker Prize with his novel *The Blackwater Lightship* (1999).

9 Frank McCourt
The evocative and tragicomic account of a tough, poverty-stricken upbringing in Limerick in his memoir *Angela's Ashes* (1996) won Frank McCourt (1930–2009) the Pulitzer Prize.

10 Tom Murphy
Murphy (b.1935) is a controversial playwright, whose work *The Wake* (1998) had a long run at the Gate Theatre (see p48).

Seamus Heaney in 1995

🔟 Historic Buildings and Monuments

City Hall's magnificent dome

grand pedimented centre with arcaded screens and triumphal arches, topped with a colonnaded rotunda and a Neo-Classical dome. The five statues by Edward Smyth on the central block represent Moses, Wisdom, Authority, Justice and Mercy.

① City Hall

A competition was held in 1768 to select the designer of the Royal Exchange, and Thomas Cooley's plans were the preferred choice. One of Dublin's most sophisticated Georgian buildings, it marked the introduction to Ireland of the Neo-Classical architectural style, with its lofty dome supported by 12 columns and its 12 elegant circular windows *(see p63)*.

② Four Courts

MAP C3 ▪ Inns Quay ▪ 01 888 6459 ▪ Open 10am–5pm in session

Designed by James Gandon in 1786, the magnificent Four Courts has a

③ Dublin Castle

Originally rectangular in shape, Dublin Castle was designed as a "keepless castle", involving four circular corner towers and, midway along the south wall, a fifth tower. However, much of the medieval castle was destroyed by fire. The remodelling that you see today began at the turn of the 18th century *(see pp18–19)*.

④ Custom House

MAP G2 ▪ Custom House Quay ▪ 01 888 2000 ▪ 2–4pm Thu, Fri; 11:30am–4:30pm Sat, Sun

Designed by James Gandon in 1791, the striking Custom House has four decorated façades, with finely balanced end pavilions and recessed Doric columns facing the River Liffey. Sculptor Edward Smyth created the fine statuary around the building. A fire destroyed much of the interior in 1921 during the War of Independence, but it was restored in the same decade. The latest superb restoration work was carried out in the 1980s.

Grand dome of the Four Courts building

The breathtaking Spire

Palladian central block, with temple and portico flanked by colonnaded wings, in 1729; James Gandon contributed the portico to the east in 1785; and Richard Parkes added the western portico. The Bank of Ireland took over the building in 1803.

8 Marsh's Library
MAP C5 ■ St Patrick's Close ■ Open 9:30am–5pm Mon, Wed–Fri; 10am–5pm Sat ■ Adm

Designed by Sir William Robinson of Kilmainham Hospital fame *(see pp32–3)* in 1701, this library was built to house the collection of Archbishop Narcissus Marsh. The Gothic-style battlements and entrance date from the 19th century, but the oak bookcases, arranged in bays between the windows, are original.

5 The Spire
The world's tallest sculpture was erected on O'Connell Street in 2002. Its hollow stainless-steel cone rises 121 m (397 ft) above the cityscape, occupying the site once dominated by Nelson's Pillar, a monument to Admiral Horatio Nelson damaged by a terrorist bomb in 1966. At night its illuminated tip becomes a beacon. Dubliners have playfully lent it many nicknames, including the "Stiletto in the Ghetto" *(see p70)*.

6 Leinster House
MAP G5 ■ Kildare St ■ Open by appt only

Designed by Richard Cassels for the Earl of Kildare in 1745, Leinster House is the home of the Irish parliament and is notable for its two contrasting façades, one resembling a town house, the other a country abode. The building was acquired by the State in 1924.

7 Bank of Ireland
MAP E4 ■ College Green

Built to accommodate the Irish House of Lords and House of Commons, the building is almost as magnificent as its English counterpart. Three archi-tects were involved in its creation: Sir Edward Lovett Pearce designed the

9 Famine Memorial
Cast in bronze by Dublin sculptor Rowan Gillespie, this haunting collection of figures staggers along Custom House Quay, from where in the 1840s thousands fled the Irish Potato Famine for a new life in North America. In all, more than a million emigrated on ships such as the *Jeanie Johnston*, moored nearby *(see p72)*.

Famine Memorial, Custom House Quay

10 GPO Building
The imposing General Post Office opened in 1814, the work of Francis Johnston. It holds a special place in Irish hearts as the spiritual birthplace of the Republic: rebels stormed the building on Easter Monday 1916, proclaiming independence *(see p68)*.

Children's Attractions

1 Dublinia
Medieval Dublin is brought vividly to life, through exhibits such as a full-size reconstruction of a merchant's house *(see p62)*.

Wax models at Dublinia

2 Zipit
MAP N5 ■ Tibradden Wood ■ 051 858 008 ■ Open Feb–Nov ■ Adm ■ www.zipit.ie
This exhilarating aerial assault course, for ages seven and up, is south of the city, near Dundrum.

3 Dublin Zoo
MAP T2 ■ Phoenix Park ■ 01 474 8900 ■ Open daily ■ Adm
Apart from the usual exotic animals there is a petting zoo, playgrounds and a train ride *(see p35)*.

4 National Aquatic Centre
Deanestown ■ 01 646 4300 ■ Open daily ■ Adm ■ www.nac.ie
In the northwestern suburbs, this mammoth facility includes an Aquazone waterpark, with slides and a wave pool.

5 National Wax Museum Plus
MAP F3 ■ Westmoreland St ■ 01 671 8373 ■ Open 10am–10pm (last entry 9pm) Mon–Sat ■ Adm
Kids will enjoy the "Children's Fantasy World", the Chambers of Horrors and models of pop idols.

6 Science Gallery
MAP G4 ■ Pearse St ■ 01 896 4091 ■ Open noon–8pm Tue–Fri, noon–6pm Sat & Sun ■ www.sciencegallery.com
Science meets art at this innovative museum located in Trinity College.

7 The Ark
MAP E4 ■ 11a Eustace St ■ Open daily ■ Adm ■ www.ark.ie
Workshops, art classes, plays, exhibitions and concerts for children.

8 Lambert Puppet Theatre
MAP U2 ■ Clifton Lane, Monkstown ■ 01 280 0974 ■ Open Sat & Sun ■ Adm ■ www.lambertpuppettheatre.ie
Performances range from fairy tales for toddlers to Yeats for older kids.

9 Imaginosity
MAP U2 ■ Sandyford ■ 01 217 6130 ■ Closed Mon am ■ Adm ■ www.imaginosity.ie
An excellent kids' museum, with three levels of interactive zones.

10 Viking Splash Tour
MAP F5 ■ Stephen's Green ■ Open mid-Feb–Nov: daily ■ Adm
A military amphibious vehicle gives you a tour on land before splashing into the Grand Canal Quay.

Viking Splash Tour

Sporting Events

Ireland in the Six Nations Rugby

1 Six Nations Rugby
MAP T2 ▪ Lansdowne Road
▪ Jan–Mar
The Aviva Stadium is the Irish venue for this annual competition.

2 Fairyhouse Racing Festival
MAP M5 ▪ Fairyhouse ▪ Easter weekend
The Fairyhouse racecourse hosts the Irish Grand National at Easter.

3 Colours Boat Race
MAP F3 ▪ First Sat in Apr
Crowds flock to the Liffey as Trinity and University College Dublin compete in the age-old rivalry of a rowing race between O'Connell Bridge and St James's Gate.

4 Women's Mini Marathon
MAP G5 ▪ First Mon in Jun
Attracting over 40,000 participants, this 10-km (6-mile) race is one of the largest all-female sporting events in the world.

5 Dublin Horse Show
MAP T2 ▪ RDS, Ballsbridge
▪ Dart Sandymount ▪ Early Aug
The Fáilte Ireland Dublin Horse Show is one of the world's top international equestrian events. It takes place over 5 days, and includes a hotly contested Ladies' Day.

6 All-Ireland Hurling Final
MAP T2 ▪ Croke Park ▪ Train Heuston ▪ First Sun in Sep
The world's oldest field sport requires a huge amount of skill to control a speeding ball (sliotar) with a hurley made of ash. It's also the world's fastest field sport, so expect lots of excitement and a bit of blood.

7 All-Ireland Football Final
MAP T2 ▪ Croke Park ▪ Train Heuston ▪ Third Sun in Sep
Gaelic football is similar to Aussie football. The pace is the same and allows carrying of the ball. The goals are divided between the net area, similar to soccer (three points), as well as rising posts (one point).

8 Laytown Races
MAP M5 ▪ Laytown
▪ Train Connolly ▪ Sep
The only Irish horse race on a beach. As the tide rolls out, the finishing posts rise and bookies open shop.

9 Dublin Marathon
MAP G6 ▪ Last Mon in Oct
Winding through the historic streets of the city the Dublin Marathon attracts thousands of spectators.

10 Leopardstown Christmas Racing Festival
MAP T2 ▪ Leopardstown ▪ 26–29 Dec
Events occur year round at Leopardstown, but the 4-day Christmas Racing Festival is one of the highlights of the Irish racing calendar. Built in 1888, the course offers some of the finest hospitality suites in racing.

Dublin Horse Show

🔟 Performing Arts Venues

The plush, grand interior of the Olympia Theatre

1️⃣ The Olympia Theatre
MAP E4 ▪ Dame St
▪ Box office: 01 679 3323

Opened in 1878 as a music hall, after years of rivalry with the Gaiety Theatre, the Olympia settled down to staging a very similar gamut of musicals and comedy.

2️⃣ Abbey Theatre
The Abbey is a legend. Founded in the early 20th century by a circle of writers including the poet W B Yeats, it gained renown at the cutting edge of Irish theatre. Controversial works by new writers such as Sean O'Casey and J M Synge were staged here, the latter causing riots on opening night. Now classics, these plays are the mainstay of the Abbey stage, while experimental work is shown on the Peacock stage *(see p70)*.

3️⃣ Project Arts Centre
MAP E3 ▪ 39 East Essex St
▪ 01 881 9613

Born as a spin-off project to the Gate, the Project Arts Centre is perhaps the most vibrant centre of performance art in the city, with a variety of young companies exploring innovative dance, music, drama and poetry. U2, Liam Neeson and Gabriel Byrne were all rising stars here.

4️⃣ The Gate Theatre
Since its founding in 1928, the Gate has been one of the most daring theatres in Europe, introducing Irish audiences to Ibsen and Chekhov and producing Oscar Wilde's *Salome* while it was banned in England. Orson Welles and James Mason began their careers here *(see p72)*.

5️⃣ National Concert Hall
MAP F6 ▪ Earlsfort Terrace
▪ 01 417 0000

This is Dublin's premier venue for quality classical music, hosting guests of the calibre of the New York Philharmonic. The building is also home to Ireland's National Symphony Orchestra. Jazz, contemporary and traditional Irish music are also performed here, and there are lunchtime concerts in summer.

The prestigious National Concert Hall

6 The Gaiety Theatre
MAP E5 ▪ S King St ▪ Box office: 01 679 5622

Dublin's oldest theatre dates from 1871. The gilded auditorium is an atmospheric backdrop for a wide range of entertainment, but, as its name suggests, the Gaiety leans more towards music and comedy.

7 Bewley's Café Theatre
MAP E4 ▪ Top Floor, Powerscourt Theatre, S William St ▪ 086 878 4001

A unique opportunity for lunchtime drama from Monday to Saturday on the top floor of Powerscourt Theatre.

Smock Alley Theatre

8 Smock Alley Theatre
MAP D4 ▪ 6–7 Exchange Street Lower ▪ 01 677 0014

Dublin's first Theatre Royal was founded in 1662 and reopened in 2012 after a bold reconstruction. It incorporates 17th-century walls in two performance spaces, and puts on a lively, mixed programme.

9 Bord Gais Energy Theatre
MAP D4 ▪ Grand Canal Square ▪ 01 677 7999

This is a fantastic venue for West End touring productions, opera, ballet, theatre and popular music.

10 The Helix
MAP T2 ▪ Collins Ave, DCU, Glasnevin ▪ 01 700 7000

This modern building at Dublin City University has a well-deserved reputation for diverse theatre, opera and music productions.

TOP 10 CULTURAL EVENTS

Cork Jazz Festival

1 Temple Bar TradFest
MAP E4 ▪ Temple Bar ▪ 01 960 2300 ▪ www.templebartrad.com ▪ Jan
Staged over 5 days, this is Dublin's biggest Irish music and culture festival.

2 Dublin International Film Festival
www.diff.ie ▪ Feb
The DIFF celebrates the best of Irish and worldwide cinema.

3 St Patrick's Festival
17 Mar
A fun 4-day series of events surrounds the parade that takes place on the day.

4 Bloomsday
16 Jun
Fans of James Joyce re-enact his novel *Ulysses* on the day it is set.

5 Great Music in Irish Houses Festival
Jun
Chamber music events are held in grand venues around Ireland.

6 Galway International Arts Festival
MAP N3 ▪ www.giaf.ie ▪ Jul
Massive annual celebration of film, theatre, art, literature and music.

7 Dublin Fringe Festival
2 weeks in Sep
The Fringe includes dance, street performances, visual arts and comedy.

8 Dublin Theatre Festival
MAP E3 ▪ 44 East Essex St ▪ 01 677 8439 ▪ Late Sep–Oct
This two-week event showcases a wealth of Irish and international talent.

9 Wexford Opera Festival
MAP P5 ▪ Oct
Performances of three different operas at Wexford's National Opera House.

10 Cork Jazz Festival
MAP Q3 ▪ End Oct
A popular festival with performances and events throughout the city.

Pubs

Kehoe's, with its old Victorian decor

1 Kehoe's
MAP F5 ■ 9 S Anne St

Just off Grafton Street, this cosy pub has lost none of its original character. It's usually busy, but there's a large snug to hide away in, just beside the entrance. Close to Trinity College, it has an engaging mix of students and old pub characters.

2 The Stag's Head
MAP E4 ■ 1 Dame Court, off Dame St

Built in 1770, the Stag's Head was refurbished in the opulent Victorian style, resembling a mix between a church and a mansion, with mirrors reaching up to the high ceiling, a counter topped with Connemara marble, plus, of course, the scary antlered namesake on the wall.

The venerable Stag's Head

3 Ryan's and F.X. Buckley
MAP T2 ■ Parkgate St ■ Train Heuston

This beautifully preserved pub with wonderful Victorian decor has self-contained snugs – originally for "the ladies" – on each side of the counter. Upstairs is a cosy restaurant which has won several awards.

4 Doheny and Nesbit
MAP G6 ■ 5 Lower Baggot Street

Close to Ireland's parliament, the Dáil, this has been a hangout for politicos and journalists for more than a century, and the Victorian ambience remains pleasingly intact.

Café en Seine's beautiful interior

5 Café en Seine
MAP F5 ■ 40 Dawson St

Decorated in French coffee-house style, the three floors of this large café-bar are filled with giant lampshades, huge mirrors, ornate sculptures and plants stretching up to a roof-height glass atrium. Expect to have to queue on weekend nights.

6 Mulligan's
MAP F3 ■ 8 Poolbeg St

Once a working-class drinking man's pub (there were originally no chairs, since "real men" should stand as they drink), Mulligan's has since attracted a mixed bag, including former US President John F Kennedy. It is still stark, but cosy nonetheless, and constantly busy.

The ancient Brazen Head pub

(7) The Brazen Head
MAP C4 ▪ 20 Lower Bridge St

This pub, in the heart of Viking Dublin, is the oldest in the country, dating back to 1198. It has served a colourful set of patriots, including James Joyce, Brendan Behan, Van Morrison and Garth Brooks. The courtyard is a lovely spot for trying out one of the best pints of Guinness in Dublin and listening to traditional Irish music.

(8) The Long Hall
MAP E4 ▪ 51 S Great George's St

Near Dublin Castle, this is very much a locals' pub, although many visitors come to experience its evocative atmosphere. The decor includes chandeliers and a pendulum clock more than 200 years old.

(9) O'Donoghue's
MAP F6 ▪ 15 Merrion Row

Music and fun are the lifeblood of this pub, which fostered the popular balladiers The Dubliners. Enjoy an informal music session, or, if the sun's shining, have a drink in the little courtyard out the back.

(10) The Porterhouse
MAP D4 ▪ 16 Parliament St

Ireland's brewing company opened its first pub brewery in Dublin in 1996. Try one of the ten beers brewed on the premises, such as Oyster stout. There's plenty of live music every night, too.

NIGHTSPOTS

1 The International Bar
One of the best drinking spots in town, with regular live music nights and comedy shows *(see p66)*.

2 The Old Storehouse
MAP E4 ▪ 3 Crown Alley
Good beer and craic, with two bands in the main bar and downstairs.

3 Copper Face Jack's
MAP E6 ▪ 29–30 Harcourt St
A lively and popular DJ club.

4 The Grand Social
MAP E3 ▪ 35 Lower Liffey St ▪ 01 874 0076
Puts on a programme of comedy, clubbing, bands and flea markets.

5 Lillie's Bordello
MAP F4 ▪ Adam Court, Grafton St ▪ 01 679 9204
You need to be a trendsetter or a celebrity to get through the door.

6 The Button Factory
MAP E4 ▪ Curved St, Temple Bar
One of the best live music venues in the city. Club nights Thu–Sun.

7 The Sugar Club
MAP F6 ▪ 8 Lower Leeson St
Great cocktails and everything from casino nights to salsa.

8 The Academy
MAP E3 ▪ 57 Middle Abbey St
Four thumping floors of music, from big-draw acts to smaller gigs.

9 Rí-Rá
MAP E4 ▪ 11 S Great George's St ▪ 01 671 1220
Relaxed yet vibrant club playing a mix of R&B, hip hop, soul, disco and electro.

10 Whelan's
MAP D6 ▪ 25 Wexford St
The bar at the back is one of Dublin's most exciting live venues.

Acoustic gig at Whelan's

🔟 Restaurants

1 Patrick Guilbaud
MAP G5 ■ **21 Upper Merrion St**
■ **01 676 4192** ■ **€€€**

This is the only two-star Michelin restaurant in Ireland and offers modern classic cuisine using Irish produce in season. Guilbaud uses Ireland's bountiful fresh fish, meat and game to create savoury Gallic dishes. The restaurant is set in one of the town houses that make up the Merrion hotel *(see p128)*. Furnished in 18th-century style, it makes a great setting for this fine cuisine.

Taste at Rustic's airy interior

2 Taste at Rustic
MAP E4 ■ **17 South Great George's St** ■ **01 526 7701** ■ **€€**

The Japanese influence at chef Dylan McGrath's Southside restaurant goes way beyond sushi and sashimi: there are five or six separate menus to mix and match, including "nabemono", a cooking style where beef and fish arrive at the table with a pot of bubbling stock, to be simmered to one's liking. The interior is airy, with lots of bare wood and high ceilings, the atmosphere buzzy and informal.

3 Mulberry Garden
MAP T2 ■ **Mulberry Lane** ■ **01 269 3300** ■ **Open Thu–Sat** ■ **€€**

It's well worth the short cab ride out to Donnybrook for this innovative little restaurant, set in a century-old cottage and ripe with Irish flavour: everything from the mineral water on the table to the art on the walls is locally sourced. The menu is fresh-from-market and changes weekly, with just three choices of starters, mains and desserts in traditional *table d'hôte* style, for €49 a head.

4 101 Talbot
A reputation for excellent, creative dishes at reasonable prices has helped 101 Talbot to become one of north Dublin's most popular restaurants. Menus feature a variety of local, European and Middle Eastern influences *(see p73)*.

5 Dax
MAP T2 ■ **23 Pembroke Street Upper** ■ **01 676 1494** ■ **€€**

It may not look all that special from the street, but in its Georgian basement Dax transports diners to a French country manor house, complete with open fire, hardwood ceilings and original flagstone floors. The food and wine are Gallic-influenced too. All in all, it's perfect for a romantic evening *à deux*.

The handsome tiled decor at popular restaurant Pichet

 Pichet
MAP E4 ■ 14–15 Trinity St
■ 01 677 1060 ■ €

The chic decor and lively atmosphere at ever-popular Pichet provide a perfect setting in which to enjoy delicious French-inspired dishes with an Irish twist, prepared by chef Stephen Gibson. The indulgent Hereford rib-eye steak béarnaise is a firm favourite. A cocktail bar adds to the vibrant ambience. The bar also serves breakfast and snacks.

Chapter One
The arched granite walls of the basement of the Dublin Writers' Museum are home to one of the city's finest restaurants. Here they serve superb authentic Irish cooking with classic French cuisine influences, including an excellent charcuterie trolley. The menu varies according to the seasonally available, locally grown organic produce. There is also a popular good-value, two-course, pre-theatre menu (see p73).

Yamamori Noodles
Established in 1995, the award-winning Yamamori Noodles is located in the heart of Dublin and offers an extensive menu of Japanese sushi and noodle dishes at very reasonable prices. There is so much to choose from that you better bring your appetite. If you find chopsticks a little daunting, ask for a fork (see p67).

Trocadero
MAP E4 ■ 4 St Andrew's St
■ 01 677 5545 ■ €€

Held in high esteem by locals and visitors alike, Trocadero is the archetypal Dublin theatre restaurant. The decor offers much to talk about with many famous stage personalities gazing down from its dark walls. Choose the excellent steak and stay late to soak up the incredible atmosphere here.

Award-winning L'Ecrivain

L'Ecrivain
MAP G6 ■ 190A Lower Baggot St ■ 01 661 1919 ■ Closed Sat lunch, Sun ■ €€

Five minutes' walk from St Stephen's Green, this extremely popular, award-winning restaurant creates original masterpieces from French-inspired dishes, accompanied by wines worthy of the food. Chef Derry Clarke and his team use fresh Irish ingredients to work the magic. It's well worth the price. Book ahead.

For a key to restaurant price ranges see p67

TOP 10 Shopping Areas

Powerscourt Townhouse's elegant 18th-century setting

1 Powerscourt Townhouse
MAP E4 ■ 59 South William St

Irish designer labels and antiques shops cluster around the indoor courtyard of this 18th-century converted town house. Products range from handmade jigsaw puzzles to antique jewellery and Irish silver. Upstairs is the Design Centre, showcasing the very best of Irish fashion. There are plenty of cafés and bars, too.

Jam Art Factory in Patrick Street

2 Jam Art Factory
MAP C5; 64 Patrick Street ■ MAP E4; 14 Crown Alley

This independent design shop has two outlets, in the dynamic Liberties district and in touristy Temple Bar. It's a mecca for imaginative jewellery, ceramics, textiles and street art – all are Irish-designed.

3 George's Street Arcade
MAP E4 ■ S Great George's St

This lovely redbrick market has shops on either side, with stalls down the centre. Exotic fruits rub shoulders with New Age baubles, fortune-tellers and vintage clothing.

4 Grafton Street
Probably the most famous pedestrian thoroughfare in Dublin, Grafton Street traditionally caters to up-market shoppers, with home-grown department stores such as Brown Thomas (see p65) and Weir's, Dublin's largest and most exclusive jeweller's, established in 1869.

5 Liberty Market
MAP B4 ■ Meath and Thomas Streets ■ Thu–Sat

Ideal for bargain-hunting, Liberty Market sells mainly fresh food and domestic goods. It's worth coming here just to soak up the atmosphere of one of the oldest areas of the city.

6 Blackrock Market
MAP T2 ■ Main St, Blackrock

A quick trip on the DART will take you to Blackrock village where, at weekends, an 18th-century tavern and courtyard host stalls selling second-hand books, clothes, jewellery and antiques.

7 Henry Street
MAP E2

The major pedestrianized thorough-fare of Henry Street is lively and buzzing, while Moore Street's out-door food market adds colour to the proceedings. Shops and department stores here tend to be better value than those south of the river. Arnotts department store, dating from 1843, is one of the city's most attractive.

8 St Stephen's Green Shopping Centre
MAP F6 ▪ St Stephen's Green

This delicate masterpiece of glass and light is a pleasant place to shop, with Irish department store Dunnes Stores, as well as international fashions from TK Maxx, Benetton and Quicksilver. The cafés here have great views of St Stephen's Green.

9 Westbury Mall
MAP E5 ▪ Balfe St

This covered walkway with its chic boutiques and cafés is a good place to escape a sudden downpour – all too common in Dublin.

10 Francis Street
MAP C4

Dublin is one of Europe's best cities for antiques, and Francis Street and the surrounding area are lined with deliciously dusty antiques shops, forming Dublin's Antiques Quarter.

An antiques shop in Francis Street

TOP 10 FOOD SELLERS

Irish Village Markets

1 Irish Village Markets
www.irishvillagemarkets.ie
These pop-up markets gather together street-food stalls, selling anything from Moorish meatballs to pad thai.

2 Temple Bar Market
MAP E4 ▪ Meeting House Sq
The sale of farmhouse cheeses, organic vegetables and similar is soundtracked by street musicians. Saturday only.

3 Moore Street Market
MAP E2
Last-chance bargains on vegetables, flowers and other fresh produce.

4 Dunne & Crescenzi
MAP F5 ▪ S Frederick St
Selling more than 100 Italian wines, fine olive oil and artisan products.

5 Sheridans Cheesemongers
MAP F5 ▪ 11 S Anne St
The best in Irish farmhouse cheese.

6 Butlers Chocolate Café
MAP E4 ▪ 24 Wicklow St
Dublin's own delicious chocolate brand, founded on Lad Lane in 1932.

7 Fallon & Byrne
MAP E4 ▪ Exchequer St
All kinds of speciality ingredients are sold at this New York-style food hall.

8 Listons
MAP E6 ▪ 25–26 Lower Camden St
More than 4,000 gourmet products are available at this enticing delicatessen.

9 Terroirs
103 Morehampton Rd, Donnybrook ▪ Bus No. 10
Discover fine wines and gourmet food.

10 Avoca Food Hall
MAP E4 ▪ 11–13 Suffolk St
Sells foodstuffs from around the world and Irish crafts in the basement.

🔟 Dublin for Free

National Gallery of Ireland

④ Park Life
Dublin abounds with green spaces, and vast Phoenix Park, originally established as a royal deer park in the 17th century, tops the bill with its free Visitor Centre housing a historical interpretation of the park through the ages, and Victorian teahouse. Farmleigh Estate, in the park's northwest corner, boasts attractive ornamental gardens, free house tours and frequent food and craft markets *(see pp34–5)*.

① Art for Free
Both the classic canvases at the National Gallery *(pp16–17)* and the cutting-edge contemporary works at IMMA *(p33)* are free to view, or else tour the eye-catching street art on North Quays and City Quay, where James Earley's massive mural is thick with Dublin landmarks.

② Free Fiddling
No trip to Dublin is complete without some traditional Irish music, whether it's a scheduled show at the Porterhouse *(see p51)*, or a turn-up-and-play shindig with the locals at M Hughes bar (19 Chancery Street). For free late-night gigs, one of the best places is Whelan's *(see p51)*.

③ A Walk Through Trinity
Strolling the cobbled quads of Trinity College can fill a morning or afternoon, especially if you stop at the free Science Gallery *(see p46)*, Douglas Hyde art gallery *(see p12)*, Old Library, home to the *Book of Kells* or Zoological Museum.

⑤ The Famine Memorial
Dublin's most moving monument is a little off the tourist track, on Custom House Quay. This unflinching family of sculptures by Rowan Gillespie remembers the victims of the 1840s potato famine, which killed a million Irish people and led a million more to emigrate, many on ships to America from the nearby docks *(see p45)*.

⑥ Free Laughs
MAP E4 ▪ 1 Dame Court ▪ 01 679 3687 ▪ www.louisfitzgerald.com
Laughs are guaranteed at the Stag's Head pub every Sunday, Monday and Tuesday night. Not only are its popular "Comedy Crunch" stand-up shows free, you get a complementary ice cream thrown in, too.

⑦ Guided Tour
www.dublinfreewalkingtour.ie
"Drink, music, literature and sex" are all on the menu on a 3-hour outing with Dublin Free Walking Tour. Its 11am trip takes in the tourist honeypots south of the river; the 3pm

Trinity College

walk heads north, off the beaten track. Both start from the Spire on O'Connell Street.

⑧ A Day at the Seaside

With its gardens, pier and breeze-blown headland hikes, Howth (see p78) is Dublin's best day by the sea. Get there on the Dart from the city centre, and dally on the harbour to watch seals sport when the fishing boats come in. Top it off with fish and chips at Beshoff's (12 Harbour Road).

Yachts docked in Howth harbour

⑨ People-Powered

Temple Bar's nerve centre for people-watching is Meeting House Square (see p22), whose vibrant Saturday food market under the umbrellas is a winner. There's a free outdoor cinema season there every summer: bag tickets from the office opposite the Photographic Archive.

⑩ See the Skulls

MAP T2 ■ **Finglas Road, Glasnevin** ■ **www.glasnevintrust.ie**
Dublin's churches are packed with fascinating memorials: romantics should try the Whitefriar Street Carmelite Church, with its relics of St Valentine. Most rewarding of all is Glasnevin Cemetery (see p76), lined with tombs of Ireland's great and good. The nearby National Botanic Gardens are free, too.

TOP 10 MONEY-SAVING TIPS

1 All Dublin's national museums, galleries and libraries are free, while most paid attractions offer about a third off ticket prices for children, students and over-60s.

2 The Dublin Pass (1, 2, 3 or 5 days) covers entry to over 25 attractions, a skip-the-queue facility and a 24-hour Hop-on Hop-off bus tour (www.dublinpass.com).

3 A special, pre-paid Leap Visitor Card will save you up to 25 percent on all bus, tram and Dart train fares in and around Dublin (www.leapcard.ie).

4 Trekker and Explorer tickets offer unlimited train travel for 4 consecutive days and any 5 days in 15, respectively (www.irishrail.ie/fares-and-tickets).

5 Intercity bus travel is cheaper still: Bus Eireann's Open Road pass gives unlimited travel on any 3 days in 6 (www.buseireann.ie).

6 Dublin Bikes offers a popular on-street rental scheme, and rides of up to 30 minutes are free. Register with a credit card at one of 100-plus bike pick-up points across the city (www.dublinbikes.ie).

7 Look out for early-bird specials at city restaurants: many offer menus for two for €20 before 7pm.

8 Trinity College lets 600 rooms in summer from under €50 (www.tcd.ie).

9 Download the free Dublin Discovery Trails app, offering five self-guided routes (www.visitdublin.com).

10 Travel off-season to save money: prices get hiked on rugby international weekends (see p47), St Patrick's Festival (see p49) and bank holidays.

Dublin Bikes for rent

Dublin and Ireland Area by Area

Ha'penny Bridge, spanning the banks of the River Liffey, Dublin

🔟 South of the Liffey

Dublin takes its name from the southwest of the city when, in prehistoric times, there was a dark pool *(Dubh Linn)* at the confluence of the River Liffey and what was once the River Poddle. The area expanded during the 18th century, when the cobbled streets of Temple Bar became a centre for merchants and craftsmen – interestingly, reverting to similar use in the 20th century. Prior to the founding of Trinity College in 1592, southeast Dublin was undeveloped. St Stephen's Green wasn't enclosed until the 1660s and it remained for private use until 1877. But from the 1850s the

A page from the Book of Kells, Trinity College

area witnessed a building boom. Today, the south is the hub of the fashionable scene, with designer stores and fine restaurants.

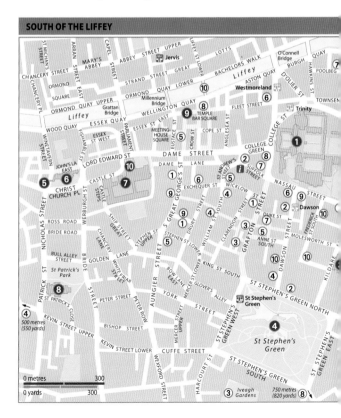

SOUTH OF THE LIFFEY

1 Trinity College

Ireland's premier institute of education was founded in 1592 by Queen Elizabeth I on the site of an Augustinian monastery. At its start, a Protestant-only college, Trinity did open its doors to Catholic students in 1793, but it wasn't until the 1970s that the Catholic Church relaxed its opposition to the college. Its quadrangles are peaceful havens, and its priceless *Book of Kells* a highlight (see pp12–13).

2 National Gallery of Ireland

An expansion to the gallery on Clare Street has vastly increased both the space available for temporary exhibitions and displays of the gallery's permanent collection. The improved facilities also include a large shop, a café and restaurant and several lecture theatres (see pp16–17).

3 National Museum of Ireland

Only two of the museum's three sites are south of the river: the Natural History Museum (see p64) and the branch on Kildare Street which examines Irish archaeology and history. The latter's 19th-century building, decorated with marble and mosaics, is almost as impressive as its collections (see pp14–15).

National Museum of Ireland

	Top 10 Sights see pp61–3
1	Places to Eat see p67
1	The Best of the Rest see p64
1	Pubs and Bars see p66
1	Southside Shops see p65

4 St Stephen's Green
MAP F6

At the foot of Grafton Street, this is downtown Dublin's primary pleasure ground, with nine hectares of land-scaped Victorian lakes and gardens, plus two miles of footpaths, a pretty waterfall, children's playground and bandstand. There are monuments to Joyce, Yeats and Wolf Tone, and a free tour of the park leaves the nearby Little Museum of Dublin at 11:30am on Saturdays and Sundays. The museum (9:30am–5pm daily; adm) is well worth a look, too – a lively sprint through the city's 20th-century history, stuffed with more than 5,000 artifacts donated by real-life Dubliners. Rock fans will enjoy the room dedicated to Irish megastars U2, on the second floor.

5 Dublinia

MAP C4 ▪ St Michael's Hill
Open Mar–Sep: 10am–6:30pm daily; Oct–Feb: 10:30am–5:30pm daily
▪ Adm

Set in the Synod Hall, part of Christ Church Cathedral *(see pp26–7)*, Dublinia brings the ancient city to life through interactive galleries, complete with sounds, smells and costumed interpreters. Experience life aboard a Viking warship before moving on to the medieval zone, with its merchant's kitchen and bustling fair. The visit ends atop St Michael's Tower, with views across Dublin.

6 Christ Church Cathedral

One of the city's two great cathedrals, illustrating the importance religion has always played in Dublin life, Christ Church was the first to be built, in 1030. Although nothing of the original wooden church now stands, there are plenty of beautiful medieval floor tiles and stone carvings. The "Treasures of Christ Church" exhibition, in the 12th-century crypt, includes a gilt plate donated by William of Orange in 1697 *(see pp24–5)*.

7 Dublin Castle

Built into the city walls in 1204, the castle was Dublin's greatest stronghold, designed to defend the British-ruled city against the native Irish. It was at that time protected by rivers on both sides, the Liffey to the north and the Poddle to the south. The castle was completely rebuilt after a fire in 1684 and was further refined during the Georgian period, from which time most of the state apartments date *(see pp18–21)*.

The nave of St Patrick's Cathedral

8 St Patrick's Cathedral

Dublin's "second" cathedral and long-time rival to Christ Church. Apart from the many monuments and plaques commemorating deceased dignitaries, and some fine architectural features, St Patrick's most interesting association is with Jonathan Swift. You can see his death mask, writing desk and chair in the north pulpit and the memorial to himself and "Stella" lies just inside the entrance *(see pp28–9)*.

Christ Church Cathedral

Temple Bar with its lively pubs

⑨ Temple Bar

This hugely popular area, on the banks of the Liffey (the term "bar" means a riverside path), is the heart of south Dublin and has a seemingly limitless array of cafés, restaurants and bars as well as interesting little shops, galleries and cultural centres, such as the Gallery of Photography and the Irish Film Institute. Its bustling, vibrant atmosphere, lively nightlife, trendy businesses and hip residents and clientele are the personification of Dublin's emergence as one of Europe's most fashionable and popular cities (see pp22–3).

⑩ City Hall

MAP D4 ▪ Cork Hill, Dame St
▪ Open 10am–5:15pm Mon–Sat
▪ Adm (for permanent exhibition)

Thomas Cooley designed this stately building between 1769 and 1779. He had won the commission as a result of a competition, beating his better-known contemporary James Gandon, who designed the Four Courts and Custom House (see p44). Cooley made a fine job of City Hall, which was originally built as the city's Royal Exchange. City bureaucrats latterly used it for various purposes but, having undergone extensive restoration in the early 2000s, it is now open to the public. There is an excellent permanent exhibition in the reconstructed vaults entitled "The Story of the Capital", covering 1,000 years of Dublin's fascinating history.

A DAY EXPLORING THE SOUTHSIDE

▶ MORNING

Have breakfast in style at **The Westbury Hotel** (see p128) then go on to spend the first half of the morning exploring the many shops on **Grafton Street** and in **Powerscourt Townhouse** (see p54) and soaking up the atmosphere of the street entertainers. Once the crowds move in, continue down to College Green and walk under the arch into **Trinity College** (see p12–13) to relax in the grounds. On leaving Trinity, head down Dame Street to **Temple Bar** (see pp22–3) and enjoy the many shops and galleries here.

For lunch, press on to Leo Burdock's, the city's oldest fish-and-chip shop (2 Werburgh St). It serves take-away only so make for **Christ Church Cathedral** (see pp24–5) and sit and admire its exterior while eating. Then wander inside to view the restored crypt and treasury.

AFTERNOON

After lunch, retrace your steps to **Dublin Castle** (see pp18–21) for a tour of state apartments and a visit to the **Chester Beatty Library**. A cup of eastern-flavoured coffee and a slice of exotic cake in the café here will set you up for the final stretch: walk west (or hop on the 123 bus) for a tour and a panoramic pint at the **Guinness Storehouse** (see pp30–31).

Finally, make for the **Brazen Head** (see p51), on Lower Bridge Street, Dublin's oldest pub, or check out an evening concert at **St Patrick's Cathedral** (see pp28–9).

See map on pp60–61 ←

The Best of the Rest

 Waterways Ireland Visitor Centre
Off MAP H4 ■ Grand Canal Quay ■ Open May–Sep 10am–6pm Wed–Sun ■ Adm

This sleek visitor centre offers enlightening walking tours.

 Government Buildings
MAP G5 ■ Upper Merrion St ■ Open Sat tours only ■ Adm

Before independence, these buildings served as the Royal College of Science.

Water feature in the Iveagh Gardens

 Iveagh Gardens
MAP E6

These little-known gardens are a lovely place to relax beside the roses.

4 Teeling Whiskey Distillery
MAP C6 ■ 13–17 Newmarket ■ Open 9:30am–5:30pm daily ■ Adm

The jaunty tours of this traditional distillery include a tutored tasting.

5 Irish Rock 'n' Roll Museum Experience
MAP E4 ■ Curved St ■ Open 11am–5:30pm daily ■ Adm

Strum a guitar and see memorabilia from U2, Thin Lizzy and more.

 **Natural History Museum**
MAP G5 ■ Merrion St ■ Open 10am–5pm Tue–Sat, 2–5pm Sun ■ Dis. access ground floor only

A remarkable collection of stuffed animals and skeletons illustrate the natural world through the ages.

7 National Library
MAP F5 ■ Kildare St ■ Closed Sunday am

With its free exhibitions (a recent one on W B Yeats won awards) and tasty café, there's much more to the National Library than just books.

8 Merrion Square
MAP G5

One of the largest and grandest of Dublin's Georgian squares, lined with stately buildings. Oscar Wilde is one of the many illustrious past residents of the square.

9 Number Twenty Nine – Georgian House Museum
MAP H6 ■ 29 Lower Fitzwilliam St ■ Closed for renovation until 2020 ■ Adm

Here's a fantastic time capsule of Georgian Dublin: a lovingly curated middle-class house dating from the 1790s, complete with all the trimmings. Guided tours run at 3pm every day.

10 Ha'penny Bridge
MAP E3

The Ha'penny Bridge was built in 1816 to link the north and south sides of the Liffey, and a halfpenny toll was once charged to cross it.

Ha'penny Bridge over the Liffey

Southside Shops

 Brown Thomas
MAP E5 ▪ Grafton St

The smartest department store in town. A couple of floors of designer labels give the fashionistas plenty of scope, and there's also a wonderful glass and china department featuring top Irish designs.

② **Hodges Figgis**
MAP F5 ▪ 56–8 Dawson St

Established in 1768, this is Ireland's oldest bookshop. The floors are full of books covering all subjects and very good bargains are available. Excellent children's section, too.

③ **Kilkenny Shop**
MAP F4 ▪ 6–15 Nassau St

The best of Irish contemporary design in fashion, art, ceramics and glass is available at reasonable prices, so it is a great place to pick up a unique souvenir.

Exterior of the Celtic Whiskey Shop

④ **Celtic Whiskey Shop**
MAP F5 ▪ 27–8 Dawson St

Choose from a vast array of local Irish whiskeys as well as more famous brands. The service is as warm as a nip of the *uisce beatha* ("water of life").

⑤ **Charles Byrne Musik Instrumente**
MAP E5 ▪ 21–22 Lower Stephen's St

From traditional instruments to novelty items like mini chocolate pianos, this family-owned shop dating to 1870 has plenty of gift ideas.

Woollen knits at House of Ireland

⑥ **House of Ireland**
MAP F4 ▪ 37–8 Nassau St

It's somewhat geared towards the tourist, but nonetheless House of Ireland sells an interesting range of Irish-made items, predominantly clothes, jewellery, gifts and Waterford Crystal *(see p87)*.

⑦ **Avoca Handweavers**
MAP E4 ▪ 11–13 Suffolk St

An Aladdin's cave with beautiful and contemporary homeware – blankets, throws and cushions – alongside gorgeous own-label fashions. There's also an excellent food section, with a restaurant on the top floor and a deli in the basement.

⑧ **James Fox**
MAP F4 ▪ 119 Grafton St

A Dublin institution, James Fox's cigarette and cigar emporium is definitely a place for connoisseurs. It specializes in Cuban and other fine cigars, plus there's an extensive range of smoking accessories.

⑨ **Kevin & Howlin**
MAP F4 ▪ 31 Nassau St

A traditional shop, with wonderful old-fashioned service, selling everything tweedy for men and women with conservative tastes, including the famous Donegal tweed.

⑩ **Designyard Gallery**
MAP F5 ▪ 25 South Frederick St

An excellent gallery shop with highly original pieces of contemporary Irish and European jewellery, sculpture and art by over 100 designers, both established and emerging.

See map on pp60–61

Pubs and Bars

① The Bar With No Name
MAP E5 ▪ 3 Fade St
▪ 087 122 1064

Tucked away behind Kelly's hotel, above the popular L'Gueuleton restaurant, is the hugely sought-after hang-out the "Secret" or "No Name Bar". It has a stylish crowd and beautiful high-ceilinged rooms.

O'Neills, a traditional old Irish pub

② O'Neills
MAP E4 ▪ 2 Suffolk St
▪ 01 679 3656

The exterior of this pub is authentic and old-fashioned, while the inside is cosy and atmospheric, with lots of different bar areas. There's a great selection of whiskeys available, too.

③ McDaids
MAP E5 ▪ 3 Harry St
▪ 01 679 4395

This pub, with stained-glass windows and wooden interior, offers literary tradition and an authentic old-style Dublin drinking experience. The writer Brendan Behan used to drink here, and it's a stop-off for a popular literary pub crawl.

④ Grogan's Castle Lounge
MAP E4 ▪ 15 South William St
▪ 01 677 9320

This friendly drinkers' joint is lined with local art, propped up by local characters, and locally feted for serving the best drop of Guinness in town. Decent toasties, too.

⑤ The International Bar
MAP E4 ▪ 23 Wicklow St
▪ 01 677 9250

Popular with writers and musicians. The evenings of live music and comedy are exceptionally good (see p51) and well-attended.

⑥ The Palace Bar
MAP E3 ▪ 21 Fleet St
▪ 01 671 7388

Right on the edge of the frantic Temple Bar, this welcoming, old-fashioned pub, built in 1823, attracts a mixed crowd of locals and tourists.

⑦ Davy Byrne's
MAP F5 ▪ 21 Duke St
▪ 01 677 5217

A friendly pub immortalized by James Joyce in his book *Ulysses*. Seafood and traditional Irish fare accompany the drink.

⑧ The Quays
MAP E4 ▪ 10–13 Temple Bar
▪ 01 671 3922

This rowdy place scores for its commitment to both traditional Irish music and food.

⑨ The Market Bar
MAP E5 ▪ 14a Fade St
▪ 01 613 9094

The benches in this vast designer bar in a former sausage factory soon fill up with people. Tasty tapas and an open kitchen add to the buzz.

⑩ 37 Dawson St
MAP F5 ▪ 37 Dawson St
▪ 01 902 2908

Expect delicious eats and tempting cocktails at this hip restaurant bar.

Places to Eat

PRICE CATEGORIES

For a three-course meal for one with half a bottle of wine (or equivalent meal), taxes and extra charges.

€ under €45   €€ €45–€90   €€€ over €90

1 Pitt Bros
MAP E4 ▪ Unit 1, Wicklow House, Georges St ▪ 01 677 8777 ▪ €

An absolute must for meat lovers, Pitt Bros is known for affordable food and generous portions. Its signature style is slow-cooked smoked meat, with brisket and pulled pork being the favourite.

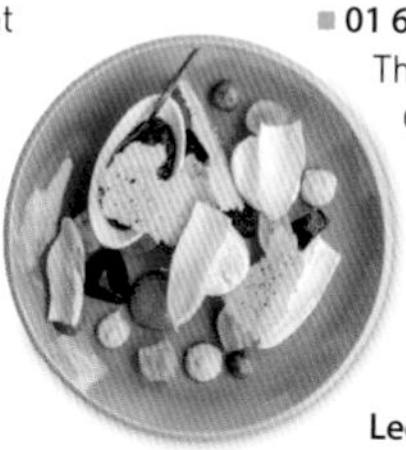

2 Peploe's Wine Bistro
MAP F5 ▪ 16 St Stephen's Green ▪ 01 676 3144 ▪ €€

Located in an elegant Georgian basement, this wine bar has a stylish atmosphere and offers snacks, as well as a rich dinner menu.

3 Bewley's Café and Restaurant
MAP E5 ▪ 78 Grafton St ▪ 01 672 7720 ▪ €

Right in the centre of Grafton Street (see p54), this iconic café opened in 1927 and has been a favourite spot for shoppers ever since.

4 The Port House
MAP E4 ▪ 64A South William St ▪ 01 677 0298 ▪ €

A little corner of Spanish heaven in the heart of Dublin – this cosy candlelit restaurant serves a wide selection of tapas to the pulse of Spanish music. Tasty, affordable fare and good, friendly service.

5 Gotham Café
MAP F5 ▪ 8 South Anne St ▪ 01 679 5266 ▪ €

This is a buzzing, New York-inspired, family-friendly pizza joint. It also serves salads, burgers and curries.

6 Fallon & Byrne
MAP E4 ▪ 11–17 Exchequer St ▪ 01 472 1000 ▪ €

This is a food-lover's haven. There is Parisian-style cuisine in the restaurant, a large ground-floor food hall and a basement wine bar.

7 Vintage Kitchen
MAP F3 ▪ 7 Poolbeg St ▪ 01 679 8705 ▪ €

This relaxed dining room does exemplary locally sourced dishes. Bring your own wine – corkage is free.

Little Kitchen

8 Little Kitchen
MAP T2 ▪ 129 Leeson Street Upper ▪ 01 669 7844 ▪ €

Breakfast, brunch, lunch and dinner are all on the menu at this chirpy place, little sister of the Vintage Kitchen.

9 Yamamori Noodles
MAP E4 ▪ 71–72 S Great George's St ▪ 01 475 5001 ▪ €

Excellent Japanese cuisine. Large portions of soups, noodles and sushi.

10 One Pico
MAP F5 ▪ 5–6 Molesworth Place, Schoolhouse Lane ▪ 01 676 0300 ▪ €€

A chic fine-dining restaurant. Try the roasted Wicklow venison loin or the John Dory with Morteau sausage.

One Pico's refined, comfortable dining room

See map on pp60–61

🔟 North of the Liffey

When Dublin was developed in the 18th century, plans for the north side of the River Liffey included a range of elegant terraces and squares designed to attract the city's elite. A downturn in the economy left the plan incomplete, although O'Connell Street and Parnell and Mountjoy squares remain evidence of what might have been. The area boasts some of the city's most beautiful buildings, such as the Custom House and the Four Courts; two theatres – the Abbey and Gate – produce drama of worldwide acclaim; and the city's great literary tradition is celebrated in the Dublin Writers' Museum and James Joyce Cultural Centre.

The Neo-Classical General Post Office

❶ General Post Office
MAP E2 ■ O'Connell St
■ Open 8am–8pm Mon–Sat

Designed in 1814 by Francis Johnston, the GPO is one of the city's most imposing buildings. It was the centre of the failed Easter Rising in 1916 and the scars of gunfire can still be seen on the Ionic portico. The history of this event is traced in a sequence of paintings in the foyer by Irish artist Norman Teeling and also in the absorbing multimedia GPO Witness History experience.

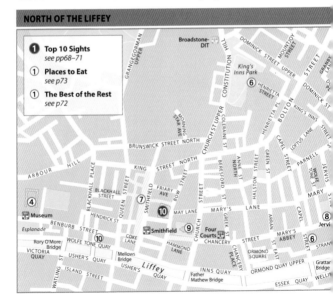

NORTH OF THE LIFFEY

❶ Top 10 Sights
see pp68–71

① Places to Eat
see p73

① The Best of the Rest
see p72

The Dublin Writers' Museum

Gallery of Writers. Downstairs, a taped commentary takes you through Irish literary history, accompanied by photographs and correspondence.

③ Parnell Square
MAP E1

The credit for this lovely Georgian square goes to Bartholomew Mosse, who founded the Rotunda Hospital here (see p72). It was considered one of Dublin's smartest addresses in the 1760s, then its fortunes declined, but it remains home to some fine literary museums and art galleries.

② Dublin Writers' Museum
MAP E1 ■ 18 Parnell Sq North ■ 01 872 2077 ■ Open 10am–5pm Mon–Sat, 11am–5pm Sun ■ Adm ■ www.writers museum.com

Rare and first editions of critical works sit alongside a collection of portraits in this original little museum. The Georgian proportions of the house are seen at their best on the upper floors, with a grand

④ James Joyce Cultural Centre
MAP F1 ■ 35 N Great George St ■ 01 878 8547 ■ Open 10am–5pm Mon–Sat, noon–5pm Sun ■ Adm ■ www.james joyce.ie

James Joyce Cultural Centre

James Joyce (see p42) spent much of his early life north of the Liffey so it is a fitting area to house a museum dedicated to the Irish writer.

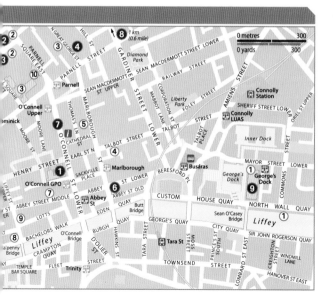

Portrait of Maud Gonne by S Purser in the Hugh Lane Gallery

NELSON'S PILLAR

In the 1880s a controversial 40-m (121-ft) column topped with a 4-m (13-ft) statue of Nelson was erected in O'Connell Street. Several attempts were made over the years to destroy this symbol of British imperialism until, in 1966, a bomb damaged it so badly that it had to be dismantled.

6 Abbey Theatre

MAP F3 ■ 26 Lower Abbey St ■ 01 878 7222 ■ www.abbey theatre.ie

The Irish National Theatre was founded at the Abbey Theatre (see p48) by the Gaelic Revival Movement led by Lady Augusta Gregory and W B Yeats (see p42) and first opened its doors in 1904. It had a radical reputation, putting on plays such as Sean O'Casey's *The Plough and the Stars*. The theatre then went into decline, before being gutted by fire in 1951. It reopened in 1966 with the Abbey stage and Peacock stage.

5 Hugh Lane Gallery

MAP E1 ■ Charlemont House, Parnell Sq North ■ 01 222 5550 ■ Open 9:45am–6pm Tue–Thu, 9:45am–5pm Fri, 10am–5pm Sat, 11am–5pm Sun ■ www.hughlane.ie

Art-lover Hugh Lane spent his life collecting art, and today the permanent collection includes exceptional 19th and 20th-century works by Irish and European artists, including Manet and Renoir. An addition is the Dublin-born painter Francis Bacon's studio.

7 O'Connell Street

MAP E2

One of the widest streets in Europe, O'Connell Street was designed by Luke Gardiner in the 1740s and was once lined with Classical buildings. Sadly, many of these were destroyed during the Easter Rising (see p39). The Monument of Light (known as the Spire) is a latter-day iconic hallmark.

Statue of Daniel O'Connell on O'Connell Street

8 Croke Park Skyline

MAP T2 ■ St Joseph's Avenue
■ 01 819 2323 ■ Tours run daily (book ahead) ■ Adm ■ www.crokepark.ie

Croke Park has a special place in Dubliners' hearts as the home of Gaelic football and hurling, their national sports. A museum fills in the history, with an interactive games zone to test visitors' ball skills, but the big draw is the "skyline tour" on the stadium roof, where guides recount stories in front of wraparound views of city, sea and mountains.

Displays at EPIC Ireland

9 EPIC Ireland

MAP G2 ■ The CHQ Building, Custom House Quay ■ 01 531 3688
■ Open 10am–6:45pm daily ■ Adm
■ www. epicirelandchq.com

This ambitious new attraction is set in the CHQ Building, an 1820s wine and tobacco warehouse. Twenty interactive galleries bring alive the story of Ireland's 10 million-strong diaspora, looking at why they left and where they ended up. There's also a state-of-the-art genealogy centre for those investigating their Irish roots.

10 Jameson Distillery Bow Street

MAP B3 ■ Bow St ■ 01 807 2355
■ Open 9am–6pm Mon–Sat, 10am–6pm Sun ■ Adm

Refurbished as a museum, the Jameson Distillery Bow Street, where whiskey was first made in the 1780s, offers a 40-minute tour that goes through the entire process of production of the Irish whiskey, from grain delivery to bottling. At the end of the tour there is a whiskey tasting.

A DAY'S STROLL AROUND THE NORTHSIDE

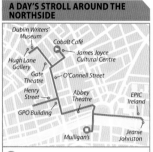

▶ MORNING

For breakfast in a lovely Georgian building head for **Cobalt Café** on North Great George Street. Across the road, the **James Joyce Cultural Centre** (see p69) is worth a peep. Afterwards, stop by the **Gate Theatre** to book tickets for the evening's performance en route to the **Hugh Lane Gallery**. Be there by 10am to have time to view the collection, then pick up the writerly thread again at the nearby **Dublin Writers' Museum** (see p69). Have lunch in the café there, and, leaving the museum, take a quick detour downstairs to **Chapter One Restaurant** (see p53 & p73) and book a table for dinner.

AFTERNOON

Cross stately **Parnell Square** and head down **O'Connell Street** to take in the **GPO Building**, perhaps devoting an hour to its striking **Witness History** exhibit (see p68). There's an optional pause for some retail therapy on neighbouring **Henry Street**, one of the city's livelier shopping districts. Then continue south to the riverside, detouring to book for the **Abbey Theatre**, if you prefer the fare on offer there for the evening.

Stroll the riverside eastwards to **Custom House Quay**, then explore the fascinating story of Irish migration at the **EPIC Ireland** attraction or aboard the **Jeanie Johnston** famine ship (see p72). Wind down with a drink in a pub, perhaps a pre-threatre pint of Guinness at **Mulligan's** (see p50), across the river.

See map on pp68–9

The Best of the Rest

The Jeanie Johnston tall ship

but St Mary's has been playing the part since 1825. It is home to the renowned Palestrina choir, who sing the Sunday morning service.

6 King's Inns
MAP C1 ■ Henrietta St, Constitution Hill ■ 01 874 4840 ■ Grounds only, open to the public

Fine Georgian buildings, designed by James Gandon in the 1790s as a training school for barristers.

7 Smithfield
MAP B3

This redeveloped cobbled area, home to horse fairs on the first Sunday of the month, is also used for concerts.

8 National Leprechaun Museum
MAP D3 ■ 1 Jervis St ■ 01 873 3899 ■ Open 10am–6:30pm daily ■ Adm

Fun for little people, this is a breezy, if slightly cheesy, celebration of Irish folklore – a crock of gold guaranteed.

9 St Michan's Church
MAP C3 ■ Church St ■ 01 872 4154 ■ Open 10am–12:45pm & 2–4:45pm Mon–Fri, 10am–4pm Sat ■ Adm

The attraction at this ancient church is the macabre mummified bodies.

10 Gate Theatre
MAP E1 ■ Parnell Square East

Converted from the 18th-century Assembly Rooms in 1928, the Gate soon made its name for high-class European productions, and today stages both new plays and classics.

1 The Jeanie Johnston
MAP G3 ■ Custom House Quay ■ 01 473 0111 ■ Open 10am–4pm (Fri–Sun only Oct–Apr) ■ Adm

This replica 1840s tall ship re-creates the squalid conditions endured by thousands of Irish voyaging to the New World.

2 Garden of Remembrance
MAP E1 ■ Parnell Sq ■ 01 821 3021 ■ Open dawn–dusk

Opened in 1966, this peaceful park commemorates all those who died in the fight for Irish Freedom.

3 Rotunda Hospital
MAP E1 ■ Parnell Sq

This was the first purpose-built maternity hospital in Europe when it opened in 1745. Inside there is a beautiful Baroque chapel.

4 Decorative Arts and History Museum
MAP A3 ■ Collins Barracks, Benburb St ■ Open 10am–5pm Tue–Sat, 2–5pm Sun

Exhibits include Soldiers and Chiefs (military history), The Way We Wore (fashion) and Irish silver.

5 St Mary's Pro Cathedral
MAP F2 ■ 83 Marlborough St ■ 01 874 5441 ■ Open 7:30am–6:45pm Mon–Sat, 9am–1:45pm & 5:30–6:45pm Sun

Catholic Dublin has not had its own cathedral since the Reformation,

The Gate Theatre

Places to Eat

PRICE CATEGORIES
For a three-course meal for one with half a bottle of wine (or equivalent meal), taxes and extra charges.

€ under €45 **€€** €45–€90 **€€€** over €90

1 Ely Bar & Brasserie

MAP H2 ■ IFSC, North Dock ■ 01 672 0010 ■ €

A lively waterside restaurant that offers a wide range of wines and delicious food made from local organic ingredients. Outdoor seating is available in summer.

2 Chapter One

MAP E1 ■ 18–19 Parnell Sq ■ 01 873 2266 ■ €€

The warm colours, comfortable seating and courteous service set the tone here. There's an excellent "pre-theatre" dinner menu *(see p71)* and Irish and French cuisine.

3 The Cobalt Café

MAP E1 ■ 16 North Great George St ■ 01 873 0313 ■ €

A bright and airy café that serves home-made soups, sandwiches and cakes, alongside an array of vegetarian stews and tarts. The walls are adorned with paintings by up-and-coming Irish artists, making Cobalt a popular haunt for art lovers.

4 101 Talbot

MAP F2 ■ 101–2 Talbot St ■ 01 874 5011 ■ €

This place is just around the corner from the Abbey Theatre. Curries and traditional classics with a modern twist are complemented by an extensive vegetarian menu.

5 Panem

MAP E3 ■ 21 Lower Ormond Quay ■ 01 872 8510 ■ Open 8:15am–5:30pm Mon–Fri ■ €

Take gorgeous filled focaccias and croissants out on to the boardwalk in the summer, or instead enjoy the chic interiors of this tiny eatery.

6 Ristorante Romano

MAP D3 ■ 12 Capel St ■ 01 872 6868 ■ €

A traditional Italian restaurant with cycling memorabilia on the walls and classics on the menu. You can expect hearty portions, friendly service and a lovely cosy atmosphere.

7 Govinda's

MAP E3 ■ 83 Middle Abbey St ■ €

This is just the place for vegetarians on a budget looking for a tasty meal.

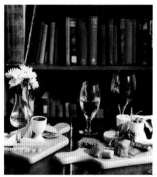

Fine Irish cuisine at the Winding Stair

8 The Winding Stair

MAP E3 ■ 40 Lower Ormond Quay ■ 01 872 7320 ■ €€

An attractively simple restaurant offering the best of Irish produce; be sure to sample the beer-braised duck.

9 Lotts Café Bar

MAP E3 ■ 9 Lower Liffey Street ■ 01 872 7669 ■ €

This antique spot, on the north side of Ha'penny Bridge, has a mosaic floor, chandeliers, and Irish steaks sizzled on a stone at your table.

10 PHX Bistro

MAP B3 ■ 12 Ellis Quay ■ 01 611 1161 ■ €

A riverside restaurant serving Irish cuisine with a twist. Try the spicy chicken wings with Cashel cheese.

See map on pp68–9 ←

🔟 Greater Dublin

The area around Dublin's city centre is rich with attractions, from stunning country estates – survivors of the Georgian heyday – to ancient Celtic remains and some spectacular scenery and walks, both in man-made landscaped surroundings and wilder natural settings. As in days gone by, many of Ireland's wealthy choose to live in Dublin County's peaceful villages, benefiting from their close proximity to the capital while enjoying a more traditional way of life. The ten sights selected here are all less than an hour's journey from Dublin.

Ship in a bottle, Maritime Museum

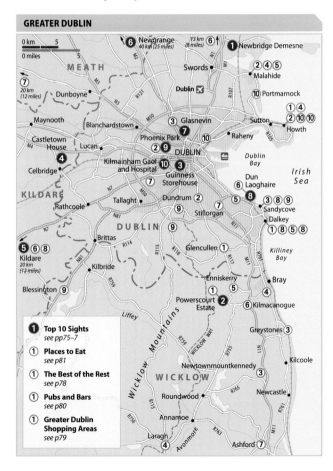

GREATER DUBLIN

1 Newbridge Demesne

MAP M5 ▪ Donabate ▪ 01 843 6534 ▪ House and farm: see website for opening hours ▪ Adm ▪ www. newbridgehouseandfarm.com

A must for architecture fans, this attractive house lies north of Dublin at the seaside village of Donabate. The house was initially designed for Archbishop Charles Cobbe in 1737 by George Semple – the Cobbe family still live in the upper half of the house although the council bought it from them in the 1980s. Rooms include the beautifully preserved Red Drawing Room, the huge kitchen and the Museum of Curiosities.

2 Powerscourt Estate

MAP T3 ▪ Enniskerry, Co Wicklow ▪ 01 204 6000 ▪ Open 9:30am–5:30pm daily (until dusk in winter) ▪ Adm ▪ www.powers court.com

Five minutes from the pretty village of Enniskerry, reached via bus from Dublin, Powerscourt Estate makes a great day trip. Visitors approach the house down a long beech-lined avenue with beautiful views across the valley. The house, designed by Richard Cassels in the 1730s, was gutted by fire in 1974, but a small exhibition gives the "before and after" story of its reconstruction. The main part of the house is now an up-market shop *(see p79)* and large restaurant. The gardens are spread over a steep slope and steps lead down to a lake.

Display at the Guinness Storehouse

3 Guinness Storehouse

To the west of the centre, this comprehensive exhibition, set in the old brewery building, takes the visitor step-by-step through the creation of the famous beer, from the grain to the final glass of creamy-topped black liquid *(see pp30–31)*.

4 Castletown House

MAP N5 ▪ Celbridge, Co Kildare ▪ 01 628 8252 ▪ Open mid-Mar–Oct: 10am–6pm daily ▪ Adm

This was the first example of Palladianism in Ireland (1722–9) and remains the most significant of its kind in the country. Architects Alessandro Galilei and Sir Edward Lovett Pearce built the house for William Conolly, Speaker of the Irish Parliament. The interiors were commissioned by Lady Louisa Lennox, wife of Conolly's great-nephew Tom, who moved here in 1758. The house remained in the family until 1965.

Panoramic views from Powerscourt Estate

The enchanting Japanese Gardens at the National Stud

5 National Stud

MAP N5 ■ **Kildare** ■ **045 521 617** ■ **Open 9am–6pm daily (last adm 5pm)** ■ **Adm** ■ **www.irishnationalstud.ie**

Visitors can tour this state-run bloodstock farm to learn about the breeding and training of these fine racehorses. The museum charts the development of the stud since its establishment by Colonel Hall Walker in 1900. Also within the estate are the Japanese Gardens, laid out between 1906 and 1910 by Hall Walker and two Japanese gardeners to represent the "life of man". St Fiachra's Garden was created to mark the Millennium and was named after a 6th-century monk with a love of gardening.

6 Newgrange and the Boyne Valley

MAP M5 ■ **Boyne Valley** ■ **041 988 0300** ■ **Opening hours vary, but always open 9:30am–5pm daily** ■ **Adm** ■ **www.newgrange.com**

Newgrange is one of the most significant passage graves in Europe (see p38). Its origins are shrouded in mystery. Built by Stone Age farmers, the circular mound contains a passage, which leads into a chamber. Visitors must pass through the excellent Brú na Bóinne Visitor Centre and join a tour. Anyone with an interest in archaeology will find the Boyne Valley fascinating, especially the ancient Hills of Tara and Slane, which feature in Celtic mythology.

Glasshouse, National Botanic Gardens

7 Glasnevin Cemetery and National Botanic Gardens

MAP T2 ■ **Glasnevin Cemetery: Finglas Road; 01 882 6550; open 9am–6pm daily; adm for museum and tours; glasnevintrust.ie.** ■ **National Botanic Gardens: Botanic Rd; 01 804 0300; open 9am–5pm Mon–Fri, 10am–6pm Sat & Sun; www.botanicgardens.ie**

Famous names interred in Glasnevin include Michael Collins, Brendan Behan, Christy Brown and Maud Gonne. Adjacent to the cemetery are the fine National Botanic Gardens.

ANCIENT OBSERVATORY

When archaeologists decided to restore Newgrange to as close to its original state as possible, they discovered that on the dawn of the winter solstice (21 December) sunlight beams through the roof on to the burial chamber, proving it to be the earliest known solar observatory.

⑧ National Maritime Museum

MAP U2 ■ Haigh Terrace, Dun Laoghaire ■ 01 280 0969 ■ Open 11am– 5pm daily ■ Adm ■ www.mariner.ie

Inspiringly arranged inside the atmospheric 180-year-old Mariners Church at Dun Laoghaire docks, this magnificent collection of engines, instruments, models and charts was revamped in 2012, and tells the story of a nation at sea. Enthusiastic and highly knowledgeable guides bring to life the history of maritime navigation, exploration, discoveries and disasters down the ages. There are also exhibits dedicated to the ill-fated *Titanic* and the *Great Eastern*, once the world's largest ship. You could end your visit at the excellent café and shop.

⑨ Phoenix Park

There is enough to see within this vast park to keep the visitor busy for a whole day. The zoo, with its elephants, is one of the main attractions, and Áras an Uachtaráin provides the official home to the President of Ireland *(see pp34–5)*.

⑩ Kilmainham Gaol and Hospital

At the far west of the city, these two institutions could not be more different. The forbidding Kilmainham Gaol, with its grim history, was restored and opened as a museum in the 1960s; in contrast, the former hospital is a fine and beautiful building, restored in the 1980s and now home to the spectacular Irish Museum of Modern Art *(see pp32–3)*.

Kilmainham Hospital

A DRIVE AROUND GREATER DUBLIN

▶ **MORNING**

Head out of Dublin on the N4 west road to Celbridge and visit **Castletown House** *(see p75)*. Take the first tour and you will get an excellent history of the house and family, as well as being talked through the architectural high-lights. Negotiate your way back to the Naas Road (N7) via Clane, across the Curragh towards Kildare and the **National Stud** – there's an excellent café here for a coffee. After a leisurely wander around the gardens, you could take the fascinating and very informative tour through the business of bloodstock.

After leaving Kildare head for **Russborough House** *(see p85)* by returning to Naas and taking the N81 Blessington road. The café-cum-restaurant at Russborough House serves simple but delicious home-made fare for lunch. After lunch, tour the house and savour the wonderful views of the **Wicklow Mountains**.

AFTERNOON

Head back to Dublin and follow signs for **Kilmainham Gaol** *(see pp32–3)*. After a somewhat sombre visit to this former prison, cut across to **Kilmainham Hospital** for the impressive Irish Museum of Modern Art. If further refreshment is required after your visit, there's a very good café in the basement. Standing in the formal gardens here, you get a great view across to the huge expanse of **Phoenix Park** *(see pp34–5)*, which you could make a visit to on your way back into the centre, energy levels permitting.

See map on p74 ←

The Best of the Rest

 Dalkey Castle and Heritage Centre
MAP U3 ▪ 01 285 8366 ▪ Castle Street, Dalkey ▪ Open 10am–5pm Wed–Mon (from 11am Sat & Sun) ▪ www.dalkeycastle.com

Dalkey's history is brought to life amid the castle ruins. You can enjoy lovely views from the battlements.

2 Howth
MAP U2

This busy fishing port offers great walks around the headland. Look out for seals when the boats come in.

 James Joyce Tower and Museum
MAP U2 ▪ Sandycove ▪ 01 280 9265 ▪ Open Apr–Aug: call for details ▪ Adm ▪ www.joycetower.ie

The first chapter of *Ulysses* (see p42) was set here and a museum contains Joyce memorabilia.

4 Killruddery House
MAP U4 ▪ Bray ▪ 01 286 3405 ▪ Visiting times vary, check website ▪ Adm ▪ www.killruddery.com

Home to the Earls of Meath, the formal gardens are the main attraction of this grand estate.

 Malahide Castle
MAP U1 ▪ Malahide ▪ 01 816 9538 ▪ Open daily ▪ Adm

With five ghosts and rounded towers, this castle has a fairy-tale quality.

6 Skerries Mills
MAP M6 ▪ Skerries ▪ 01 849 5208 ▪ Open 10am–5.30pm ▪ Adm ▪ www.skerriesmills.org

This seaside enclave has been stone-grinding flour for at least 500 years, and its windmills and water-mill make an enlightening day out.

 Drimnagh Castle
MAP T2 ▪ Long Mile Road, Dublin 12 ▪ 01 450 2530 ▪ Open 9am–4pm Mon–Fri ▪ Adm ▪ www.drimnaghcastle.org

The only Irish castle still hemmed by a flooded moat, Norman Drimnagh has a restored great hall and 17th-century gardens.

8 Killiney Hill Park
MAP U3 ▪ Co Dublin

It is worth the climb here for the spectacular views over Dublin Bay.

9 St Enda's Park
MAP T2 ▪ Grange Road, Rathfarnham ▪ 01 493 4208

One of Dublin's more charming parks, with riverside walks, follies, a waterfall and walled garden.

10 Casino Marino
MAP T2 ▪ Off Malahide Rd, Marino ▪ 01 833 1618 ▪ Open mid-Mar–Oct: 10am–5pm daily ▪ Adm

Built in the 1750s, the casino is considered among the finest Neo-Classical buildings in Europe.

Malahide Castle

Greater Dublin Shopping Areas

1 Powerscourt
MAP T3 ■ Powerscourt House, Enniskerry

Spread over two floors of the main house *(see p75)* are numerous different outlets. Avoca is the main retailer but there are plenty of others, including Waterford Crystal and Global Village interiors. The garden centre is also excellent.

Dundrum Town Centre shops

2 Dundrum Town Centre
MAP T2 ■ Dundrum

Said to be Ireland's largest shopping centre, the massive Dundrum Centre has over 160 shops, including Harvey Nichols and House of Fraser, as well as a cinema, restaurants and a theatre.

3 Fishers of Newtownmountkennedy
MAP U4 ■ The Old Schoolhouse, Newtownmountkennedy ■ 01 281 9404 ■ www. fishers.ie

Tucked away in a rather unlikely spot is this family-run place, selling up-market women's fashions and traditional men's country clothes.

4 Malahide
MAP U1

An extremely attractive village with its streets arranged in a cross-grid pattern. There are a variety of shops to visit, including an excellent wine shop, designer boutiques and a well-stocked hardware store.

5 Dalkey
MAP U3

Another pretty seaside village, and the home of many international stars. There are a couple of excellent galleries as well as designer boutiques selling pure linen clothes and original silk knitwear.

6 Avoca Handweavers
MAP U3 ■ Kilmacanogue, Co Wicklow ■ 01 274 6900 ■ www. avoca.ie

The flagship Avoca store stocks a wide range of own-label clothes, gifts and foods. The self-serve restaurant sells huge helpings of Mediterranean food.

7 Mount Usher Gardens
MAP U5 ■ Ashford

This arcade of shops includes French label casual wear, equestrian clothes and equipment, an ice-cream parlour, art gallery and a pottery.

8 Kildare Village
MAP N5 ■ Nurney Road, Kildare town ■ 045 520 501

This outlet shopping centre sells discounted designer brands. There are plenty of nice cafés if you need a break from the shops and an express bus runs from Dublin Airport.

9 Glasthule and Sandycove
MAP U2

These two pretty seaside villages sit alongside each other and are packed with boutiques and food sellers. Caviston's Food Emporium on Glasthule Road is a real delight.

10 Wrights of Howth
MAP U2 ■ 14 West Pier, Howth ■ 01 816 7347

Right on the pier, Wrights has a great selection of fresh fish – try the wild smoked salmon or gravlex.

See map on p74

Pubs and Bars

Atmospheric Johnnie Fox's pub

1 Johnnie Fox's
MAP T3 ■ Glencullen
■ 01 295 5647 ■ www.jfp.ie

A well-known and respected pub, 5 km (3 miles) from Enniskerry. The 18th-century inn is full of old beams and roaring open fires, and has a seemingly endless series of rooms.

2 Wrights Anglers Rest
MAP S2 ■ Strawberry Beds
■ 01 820 4351 ■ www.theanglersrest.ie

Boasting a lovely outdoor patio in summer and an open fire in winter, this cosy pub serves a range of beers and wines, along with great food.

3 John Kavanagh
MAP T2 ■ 1 Prospect Square, Dublin 9 ■ 01 830 7978

Well placed for a bite while visiting Glasnevin Cemetery and the National Botanic Gardens *(see p76)* – hence its nickname the Gravediggers – this old-school pub dates from 1833.

4 Lynhams Laragh Inn
MAP T5 ■ Laragh, Co Wicklow ■ 0404 45345
■ www.lynhamsoflaragh.ie

A wonderful, welcoming pub with hearty fires and a jolly crowd of locals, just east of Glendalough.

5 The Purty Kitchen
MAP U2 ■ 3–5 Old Dunleary Rd, Monkstown ■ 01 284 3576
■ www.purtykitchen.com

Top-notch seafood within a stone's throw of Monkstown's seafront.

6 The Silken Thomas
MAP N5 ■ Kildare
■ 045 522 232

This is both pub and restaurant and produces excellent and reasonably priced bar food. It is named after the fancy attire worn by Thomas Fitzgerald, famous for his rebellion against King Henry VIII in the mid-16th century *(see p18)*.

7 James Griffin Pub
MAP M5 ■ High St, Trim, Co Meath ■ 046 943 1295

An award-winning traditional pub in the pretty town of Trim, this place is a real institution. The warm and lively atmosphere makes this an ideal place to grab a pint of Guinness after a visit to the beautiful Trim Castle. There is regular live Irish music.

8 The Queens Bar and Steakroom
MAP U3 ■ Castle St, Dalkey, Co Dublin
■ 01 285 4569

A mid-18th-century public house in south Dublin's Dalkey village with open fires and wholesome pub grub.

9 The Merry Ploughboy Pub
MAP T3 ■ Rockbrook, Edmondstown Rd, Rathfarnham ■ 01 493 1495

If you're looking for traditional music, song and Irish dancing, head to Rathfarnham, near the Dublin mountains, for a night of Irish charm.

10 Abbey Tavern
MAP U2 ■ 28 Abbey St, Howth
■ 01 839 0307

There's a great atmosphere in this 16th-century inn, which makes the most of its antique features. It hosts regular traditional Irish evenings.

Places to Eat

1 King Sitric
MAP U2 ■ East Pier, Howth
■ 01 832 5235 ■ €€

At the end of Howth's harbourfront is this respected restaurant. The freshest local seafood is on offer in comfortable surroundings. There are good views from the first floor. Reservations are essential.

2 Bon Appetit
MAP U1 ■ 9 James Terrace, Malahide ■ 01 845 0314 ■ €€

The Michelin-starred chef here, Oliver Dunne, developed his skills working for Gary Rhodes and Gordon Ramsey.

3 Hungry Monk
MAP U4 ■ Church Rd, Greystones ■ 01 287 5759 ■ €

This quirky but high-quality restaurant specializes in game in winter and fish dishes in summer.

Aqua Restaurant with its sea views

4 Aqua Restaurant
MAP U2 ■ 1 West Pier, Howth, Co Dublin ■ 01 832 0690 ■ €€

In a picturesque location on a pier in Howth fishing village, Aqua serves excellent Continental cuisine including, of course, seafood.

5 Poppies
MAP T3 ■ The Square, Enniskerry ■ 01 282 8869 ■ €

A cottage-style place resembling an English tearoom. Generous portions of home cooking.

PRICE CATEGORIES

For a three-course meal for one with half a bottle of wine (or equivalent meal), taxes and extra charges.

€ under €45   €€ €45–€90   €€€ over €90

6 Hartley's
MAP U2 ■ 1 Harbour Rd, Dun Laoghaire ■ 01 280 6767 ■ €

A very special restaurant in what used to be the Customs Hall. There's lots of space and light, with high ceilings and attractive decor. The seafood menu is delicious.

7 Riba
MAP T2 ■ 4 Lower Kilmacud Rd, Stillorgan ■ 01 288 1999 ■ €

Stillorgan's "Magic Chef" chip shop has been reborn as this rather smart bistro, serving dry-aged sirloins, superfood salads and a daily "brunch spectacular".

8 Cavistons
MAP U2 ■ 59 Glasthule Rd, Sandycove ■ 01 280 9120 ■ €

This small, smart restaurant has a reputation for producing mouth-watering fish dishes. It is open for lunch with three sittings, and also for dinner on Friday and Saturday.

9 Grangecon Café
MAP S3 ■ Lake Rd, Blessington, Co Wicklow ■ 045 857 892 ■ €

Everything is home-made and the locally sourced ingredients are all organic at this café serving simple and tasty food. It also does delicious take-away breads and cakes. Open for lunch only.

10 The Osborne Brasserie
MAP U1 ■ Portmarnock Hotel and Golf Links, Strand Rd, Portmarnock ■ 01 846 0611 ■ €

Named after the Impressionist artist Walter Osborne, this hotel restaurant offers spectacular views of Dublin Bay. The good-value food is very hearty with an emphasis on seafood.

See map on p74

Wicklow Mountains

The rugged beauty of the Wicklow Mountains, seen from Wicklow Gap

1 Wicklow Gap
MAP S5

This atmospheric spot is on the R756 road. From here, it's a boggy hike up to the 2,670-ft (816-m) Tonelagee viewpoint, for breathtaking views of the lonely beauty of the Wicklow Mountains. Another worthwhile stop is the Sally Gap, a remote crossroads on the R115 road. In times past, its bogs were a favourite hideout for Irish warriors and rebels.

Glendalough monastic site

2 Glendalough
**MAP S5 ■ County Wicklow
■ 040 445 325 ■ Open daily**

A large part of the charm of this important monastic site is its location. The name translates as "the valley of the two lakes": the Upper Lake provides some of the most splendid scenery, with wooded slopes and a plunging waterfall, while the Lower Lake is surrounded by monastic ruins. St Kevin, a member of the Leinster royal family, founded the monastery in the 6th century and it became a renowned centre of Celtic learning.

3 Wicklow Way
MAP S5

For visitors who really want to see the mountains at close hand, there's nothing better than walking. Numerous easy, marked local paths run through pretty hill country, while the Wicklow Way is more demanding and for serious hikers. This 79-mile (127-km) marked path, taking around 9 days, makes its way through the heart of the region, all the way from Dublin to Clonegal, in County Carlow.

4 Clara Lara Fun Park
MAP T5 ■ Open May: Sat & Sun; Jun–Aug: daily

A top recreation site for families, the Fun Park is in the Vale of Clara, and near the village of Laragh – hence the name. Its rides are mostly based around water, but there are Go Karts, too, and the highest slide in Ireland, as well as tree-houses, climbing frames and picnic areas.

Previous pages The Giant's Causeway, Northern Ireland

5 Avondale Forest Park
MAP T6 ▪ Rathdrum ▪ 040 446 111 ▪ Open Apr–Sep: Thur–Sun ▪ Adm

Charles Stewart Parnell *(see p39)* was born in Georgian Avondale House, which is now a museum to his memory. Beautiful Avondale Forest Park has waymarked trails, some along the bucolic River Avonmore, and there's an 18th-century arboretum to discover.

6 Devil's Glen
MAP U5

Although close to Wicklow Town, this romantic wooded glen, with its waterfall and chirruping birds, is a haven of peace and tranquillity. It is part of the pretty valley of the Vartry. Perfect for walking or riding, it makes a quiet escape within an hour's drive of Dublin. There are many pleasant self-catering apartments and small cottages to rent, as well as stables and other facilities.

7 Vale of Avoca
MAP U3

"There is not in the wide world a valley so sweet," wrote 19th-century poet Thomas Moore in his work *The Meeting of the Waters*. It is perhaps not quite as idyllic now as it was then, but the meeting of rust-coloured rivers among wooded hills is still enticing. Avoca Handweavers, at the nearby village *(see p79)*, produces wonderful authentic tweeds in Ireland's oldest handweaving mill.

8 Russborough House
MAP N5 ▪ Mar–Dec 10am–6pm ▪ Adm ▪ www.russborough.ie

Russborough House holds the famous Beit Art Collection. Nearby, the River Liffey has been dammed to form a picturesque reservoir.

Mount Usher Gardens, Ashford

9 Mount Usher Gardens
MAP U5 ▪ Ashford ▪ 040 440 205 ▪ Open 10am–6pm daily ▪ Adm

Set in a sheltered valley at Ashford, northwest of Wicklow town, these fine "Robinsonian" gardens combine a distinguished collection of trees and shrubs and informal floral planting. A tree trail guide directs visitors to the show-stoppers.

10 Wicklow Town
MAP U5 ▪ Wicklow Gaol: open mid-Apr–Sep: 10am–6pm daily; adm; www.wicklowshistoricgaol.com

Wicklow's modest county town has a low-key charm, with its harbour and unpretentious pubs. The one unmissable sight is Wicklow Gaol. A shocking tale is told at this notorious jailhouse (closed in 1924), where hundreds of Irish rebels were detained, often tortured and, in many cases, hanged. Evocative exhibitions fill in the background, and include a section on the deportation of the inmates to colonies, such as Australia.

The charming marina at Wicklow Town

🔟 Around Waterford

Green and hilly County Waterford is exposed to the Atlantic to the south, the beautiful Blackwater and Suir rivers penetrate far inland, while Waterford City stands by an excellent natural harbour. All these factors made this corner of the southeast almost too welcoming to outsiders – Waterford City (Vadrafjord in Norse), founded in AD 853, is thought to be the oldest surviving Viking town in Europe. Later, Normans also chose this spot for their first Irish settlement. In few other places can Celtic, Norse and Norman relics be found so close to one another. In modern times, Waterford has been staunchly patriotic and proud of its heritage – it even has a small *Gaeltacht* (Irish-speaking district) around the village of Rinn.

The fishing village of Dunmore East

① Dunmore East
MAP Q5

A working fishing harbour with brightly coloured boats, and little cottages set among woods, this attractive village has some excellent seafood restaurants and traditional pubs and is a favourite outing for a drink, lunch or a waterfront stroll. Many of the cottages are available for holiday lets. Nearby sandy coves include the popular Lady's Cove beach, and there are several enjoyable marked walks and hikes.

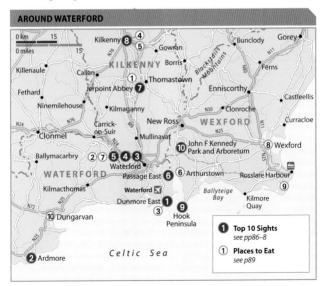

AROUND WATERFORD

① Top 10 Sights
see pp86–8

① Places to Eat
see p89

The sweeping sandy bay at Ardmore

② Ardmore
MAP Q4

Modern Ardmore is a popular little beach resort. The hill behind is the site of St Declan's 5th-century monastery, probably the oldest in Ireland. Its many evocative remains (mostly dating from the 12th century) include St Declan's Cathedral, a fine example of a high cross, and a 30-m (100-ft) round tower.

③ House of Waterford Crystal
MAP Q5 ▪ The Mall, Waterford City ▪ 05 131 7000 ▪ Open Mar–Oct: 9am– 4:15pm daily; Nov–Feb: 9:30am– 3:15pm Mon–Fri ▪ Adm for tour

The Waterford Crystal factory, for many years a major source of employment and local pride, is now located in a grand old building which used to house the electricity board. About 53,000 pieces are created here annually by specialist glassblowers and cutters. Tours of the factory are available, and there is a retail store and a café.

④ Waterford City Centre
MAP Q5

Surviving sections of Waterford's city walls show clearly the limits of the original Viking settlement, also bordered on one side by the River Suir. Today, that waterfront, with its lively and attractive quays, is the focal point of the town. The 18th-century City Hall houses important local memorabilia The city is famous for its glassworks.

⑤ Waterford Treasures
MAP Q5 ▪ Waterford ▪ 051 849 501 ▪ Open daily ▪ Adm

These three museums, located in Waterford city, document over 1,000 years of history. Reginald's Tower houses the Treasures of Viking Waterford, a collection of artifacts that tell the story of the city's Viking heritage. An exhibition on medieval Waterford is displayed in Choristor's Hall, and the Georgian era is represented in the former Bishop's Palace, home to the oldest piece of Waterford crystal in the world – a decanter from the 1780s.

⑥ Passage East
MAP Q5

A small, enjoyable ferry plies back and forth across Waterford Harbour from this peaceful, scenic waterside village, with its handful of painted cottages. It was at this spot that the Normans arrived in Ireland in 1170 and their sturdy stone tower still stands guard over the harbour.

The harbour at Passage East

Stone carvings in Jerpoint Abbey

7 Jerpoint Abbey

MAP P4 ▪ Thomastown
▪ 05 6772 4623 ▪ Open Mar–Sep: 9am–5:30pm daily; Oct: 9am–5pm daily; Nov: 9:30am–4pm daily; Dec–Feb: pre-booked tours only ▪ Adm

One of Ireland's best examples of a Cistercian monastery, the restored chapterhouse and part of the cloisters of 12th-century Jerpoint stand grandly among its ruins in a peaceful countryside setting. The Jerpoint community established itself as a centre of culture and learning, and was very prosperous until the Dissolution in 1540, when it was surrendered to the Crown. Many fine pieces of stone-carving can be seen, and there is a useful Interpretative Centre.

8 Kilkenny

MAP P4

Rapidly staking a claim as a foodie capital thanks to its clutch of crea-tive restaurants, some with Michelin stars, Ireland's medieval capital is a civilized and worthwhile stopping point. Its Norman castle looms impressively over the River Nore, and the old stable block has been converted into a hub for Irish

arts and crafts. The city's rewarding medieval remnants include St Canice's Cathedral and late 16th-century Rothe House, which now hosts the Kilkenny History Museum, containing a number of archaeological artifacts.

9 Hook Peninsula

MAP Q5 ▪ Tintern Abbey: open mid-May–Sep: 10am–6pm daily; adm

The peaceful "Ring of Hook" headland lies beside the broad Waterford Harbour, with long sandy beaches, rugged cliffs and many relics of the past. At the northeast corner, ruined Tintern Abbey – with its beautiful grounds and riverside setting – was founded in 1200 and, although much altered and restored, remains atmospheric. The peninsula's wild tip, where there has been a lighthouse since the 5th century, is beloved of bird-watchers.

Partially restored Tintern Abbey

10 John F Kennedy Park and Arboretum

MAP P5 ▪ New Ross ▪ Open 10am–dusk daily ▪ Adm

Some 4,500 international species of trees and shrubs – all carefully labelled – grow in this delightful 600-acre arboretum, created in memory of the former US president. You can visit the Kennedy Homestead in New Ross and see the birthplace of his great-grandfather.

Places to Eat

 Lady Helen Restaurant
MAP P5 ▪ Mount Juliet, Thomastown ▪ 056 777 3000 ▪ €€

This is one of the region's more sophisticated restaurants and serves an imaginative menu with international influences. It has one Michelin star and three AA rosettes.

② **Bianconi**
MAP Q5 ▪ Granville Hotel, Waterford ▪ 051 305555 ▪ €

Overlooking the quayside, this award-winning hotel restaurant serves the best of contemporary, Italian-influenced cuisine.

③ **Three Sisters Inn**
MAP Q5 ▪ Dunmore East ▪ 051 385314 ▪ €

The award-winning menu at this excellent restaurant is strong on freshly caught local seafood.

④ **Rinuccini**
MAP P4 ▪ 1 The Parade, Kilkenny ▪ 056 776 1575 ▪ €€

This multi-award-winning family-run restaurant serves classic Italian dishes and the best of modern Irish cooking in an intimate setting.

⑤ **Campagne**
MAP P4 ▪ Gas House Lane, Kilkenny ▪ 056 777 2858 ▪ €€

Michelin-starred chef-patron Garrett Byrne fuses French and Irish influences; try the saddle of hare with quince and red wine.

PRICE CATEGORIES

For a three-course meal for one with half a bottle of wine (or equivalent meal), taxes and extra charges.

€ under €45   €€ €45–€90   €€€ over €90

⑥ **The Harvest Room at Dunbrody Country House**
MAP P5 ▪ Arthurstown ▪ 051 389600 ▪ €€

Owner Kevin Dundon is regarded as one of Ireland's finest cooks, and the restaurant in this fine country-house hotel is elegant, with outstanding food and an excellent wine list.

⑦ **La Bohème**
MAP Q5 ▪ 2 George's St, Waterford ▪ 051 875645 ▪ €

This elegant French restaurant near the river Suir is housed in the vaults of a historic building. It has bright decor and the contemporary menu offers modern delicacies.

⑧ **Greenacres Bistro**
MAP P5 ▪ Selskar, Wexford ▪ 053 912 2975 ▪ €

An attractive Italian restaurant with its own art gallery, Greenacres Bistro is popular for its delicious food and the exceptional wine list.

⑨ **The Lobster Pot**
MAP P5 ▪ Carnsore Point, Carne ▪ 053 913 1110 ▪ €

Situated near the sea and prettily decorated with hanging baskets, this cheerful pub-restaurant serves very fine seafood.

⑩ **The Tannery**
MAP Q4 ▪ 10 Quay St, Dungarvan ▪ 058 45420 ▪ €

Don't miss out on chef Paul Flynn's award-winning modern Irish cuisine, which uses local ingredients. There is also a cookery school here.

Campagne's cool, art-filled interior

See map on p86

📺 The Ring of Kerry and the Dingle Peninsula

The southwest of Ireland is one of the most beautiful regions of the country. The Killarney National Park is an experience in itself but, if at all possible, like the Ring of Kerry, it should be seen off-season – the area has become so popular that driving the Ring can turn into a nightmare of tour buses in high season. The area is largely made up of peninsulas: the stunning Dingle Peninsula to the north, Iveragh, the largest, in the middle, and the most popular, the Beara Peninsula, with two impressive mountain ranges running along its spine, offering wonderfully dramatic views. Amid this landscape are some striking Georgian residences, pretty villages and ancient religious sites.

Puffins on Skellig Michael

① Valentia Island and the Skelligs

MAP Q1 ▪ Co Kerry

The Skellig Experience visitor centre, near the causeway linking Valentia Island to the mainland, includes exhibits on the history of the Skellig

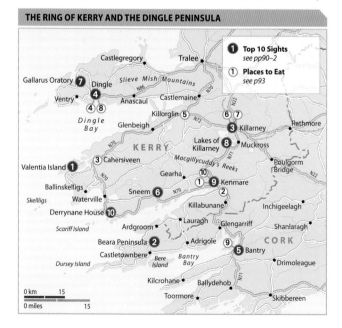

THE RING OF KERRY AND THE DINGLE PENINSULA

- ① **Top 10 Sights**
  see pp90–2
- ① **Places to Eat**
  see p93

0 km 15
0 miles 15

Fishing boats in the fine natural harbour at Dingle

Michael monastic site and a range of information on local flora and fauna. Valentia is a popular holiday spot and is particularly good for water sports, but the only inhabitants of the Skelligs now are the birds. Cruises circle the islands but do not land.

2 Beara Peninsula
MAP R1 ■ Co Cork and Co Kerry

With its pretty villages, beaches, mountains and walking trails, the Beara Peninsula has something for everyone. The two ranges here are the Slieve Miskish and Caha Mountains. Tortuous bends wend their way to the summits, but it's worth it for the view on fine days. If you are interested in wildlife, it's well worth taking the cable car across to Dursey Island, with its seabird colonies.

3 Killarney
MAP Q2 ■ Co Kerry

On the doorstep of the Ring of Kerry, with a wealth of excellent hotels, great pubs with traditional Irish music, and old-fashioned ponies and traps, it's not surprising that this attractive town becomes inundated with visitors in summer. The numerous gift shops and restaurants are worth the visit, but the real draw is the beautiful surrounding scenery of lakes, mountains and woodland.

4 Dingle
MAP Q1 ■ Co Kerry

A small, attractive fishing town with a fine natural harbour, Dingle is extremely popular with tourists, who appreciate its charm. Fungie the dolphin is the town's most famous resident and people come for miles to see him play in the harbour.

Bantry House at the head of Bantry Bay

5 Bantry Bay and Bantry House
MAP R1 ■ Bantry, Co Cork ■ Bantry House: open Apr–Oct: 10am–5pm Tue–Sun; adm; www.bantryhouse.com

This market town and fishing port is named after its beautiful situation at the head of Bantry Bay. Bantry House, owned by the White family since 1739, commands outstanding views across the bay and has stunning gardens and a lovely tearoom.

6 Sneem
MAP Q1
■ Co Kerry

This pretty, popular village, backed by the 684-m (2,244-ft) Knockmoyle Mountain, resembles something out of a children's picture book, with its houses all painted different colours.

7 Gallarus Oratory
MAP Q1 ■ Ballydavid, Co Kerry ■ Visitor centre: 066 915 5333

The best preserved early Christian site in Ireland is believed to have been built some time between the 7th and 8th centuries. Local legend has it that if you climbed out of the oratory window your soul would be cleansed – an impossible task, since the window is about 18 cm (7 in) long and 12 cm (5 in) wide.

The serenely beautiful Upper Lake, Killarney

8 Lakes of Killarney
MAP Q2 ■ Killarney, Co Kerry

The three lakes in this region, Upper, Middle (Muckross) and Lower (Lough Leane), are linked by the Long Range channel and are all incorporated into the stunning 103-sq-km (40-sq-mile) Killarney National Park. Flanked by mountains, and with a varied landscape of woodland, heather and peat bogs, the area offers a range of beautiful walks and drives.

9 Kenmare
MAP Q2 ■ Co Kerry

This prosperous town, designed by the Marquis of Lansdowne in 1775, has more of a continental atmosphere than an Irish one, with its smart shops and fine restaurants. The town's greatest claim to fame, however, is more traditional – as a centre of lacemaking.

10 Derrynane House
MAP Q1 ■ Co Kerry ■ 066 947 5113 ■ Adm

Derrynane is a lovely spot on the coast with 3 km (2 miles) of dunes and beaches. Derrynane House is 3.5 km (2 miles) from Caherdaniel and is set in 120 hectares (300 acres) of beautiful parkland. It was the family home of Catholic politician and lawyer Daniel O'Connell (see p39). It has been sensitively restored and now contains an interesting museum dedicated to the Great Emancipator.

The simple stone Gallarus Oratory

THE SKELLIGS

The history of the Skellig Islands dates back to the 6th century when St Fionán founded the monastery of Skellig Michael. All that remains now are the ruins of the church, two oratories and six beehive cells perched on a narrow platform. From 1821 to as recently as 1981, the lighthouses here were looked after by solitary lighthouse keepers. Skellig Michael was designated a World Heritage Site in 1996.

Places to Eat

(1) Packies
MAP Q2 ▪ Henry St, Kenmare
▪ 064 664 1508 ▪ Closed Sun & Nov–
Easter ▪ €€

Relaxed and informal, the hallmark of this restaurant is simplicity and purity of ingredients – superfresh fish and shellfish and organic produce.

(2) Sheen Falls Lodge
MAP Q2 ▪ Kenmare, Co Kerry
▪ 064 664 1600 ▪ €

Everything about this hotel is grand. The La Cascade restaurant is no exception and the food is faultless.

(3) QC's Seafood Bar & Restaurant
MAP Q1 ▪ 3 Main St, Cahersiveen
▪ 066 947 2244 ▪ €

This delightful old bar is full of character. It has a nautical theme which extends to the menu – there's plenty of tasty, chargrilled seafood.

(4) The Charthouse Restaurant
MAP Q1 ▪ The Mall, Dingle ▪ 066 915 2255 ▪ Open daily in summer, call for winter times ▪ €

This informal modern restaurant is to the east of town with windows overlooking the harbour. The food combines many flavours, with both Asian and European influences.

(5) Nick's Restaurant
MAP Q2 ▪ Lower Bridge St, Killorglin, Co Kerry ▪ 066 976 1219 ▪ €

This is an award-winning seafood restaurant and gastro bar, popular with the locals, with generous portions of traditional dishes.

(6) Gaby's Seafood Restaurant
MAP Q2 ▪ 27 High St, Killarney, Co Kerry ▪ 064 663 2519 ▪ €€

Run by the Maes family, who have been in the business for decades, Gaby's is definitely one of the best fish restaurants in town.

PRICE CATEGORIES
For a three-course meal for one with half a bottle of wine (or equivalent meal), taxes and extra charges.
....
€ under €45   €€ €45–€90   €€€ over €90

(7) Jam
MAP Q2 ▪ Old Market Lane, Killarney, Co Kerry ▪ 064 663 7716 ▪ €

This popular café, with plenty of seating, also has branches in Kenmare and Cork. Expect imaginative lunches using local produce.

(8) The Half Door
MAP Q1 ▪ John St, Dingle, Co Kerry ▪ 066 915 1600 ▪ €

This cottage-kitchen restaurant is famed for its generous seafood platters in lemon butter.

(9) Bantry House
MAP Q2 ▪ Bantry, Co Cork
▪ 027 50047 ▪ €

This fine house (see p91) overlooking Bantry Bay has an excellent tearoom.

(10) The Lime Tree
MAP Q2 ▪ Shelburne St, Kenmare ▪ 064 664 1255 ▪ €€

Widely acclaimed, friendly and charming, The Lime Tree serves delicious meals prepared using local produce. Try, for example, the Skeaghanore free-range duck with rhubarb and ginger chutney.

Dining room at The Lime Tree

See map on p90

TOP 10 Around Cork

Cork city and the surrounding area are full of historic, cultural and scenic places to visit. Cork itself is a lovely city, worth 1 or 2 days' exploration, including several islands in Cork harbour formed by the two sections of the River Lee. Cobh, situated on what is known as Great Island, came into its own in the 19th century as an important naval base, owing to its huge natural harbour. Between Cork and Youghal, the small town of Midleton boasts one of the oldest distilleries in Ireland, Jameson, home to the famous Irish whiskey. The equally well known Blarney Castle, with its "magic" stone, is only a short trip to the north of Cork. To the south, Kinsale is a charming fishing village, a good base for exploring the area.

Panoramic view of Cork City, seen from St Patrick's Hill

AROUND CORK

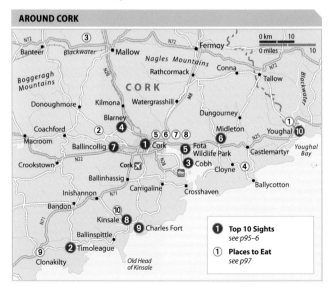

1 Top 10 Sights
see p95–6

1 Places to Eat
see p97

1 Cork City
MAP Q3

Officially Ireland's second city, Cork is a true rival to Dublin according to its 120,000 local residents. Set on an island in the River Lee, the picturesque quays north and south of the river, linked by an array of bridges, offer spectacular views. The waterways, narrow alleys and Georgian buildings, together with the balmy climate, lend the city a more Continental than Irish atmosphere.

2 Timoleague Abbey
MAP R3 ▪ Timoleague

A bleak atmosphere pervades this ruined 13th-century Franciscan abbey, especially when the mist hangs over it. Of particular interest is the wine cellar – the friars imported Spanish wines in the 16th century.

3 Cobh
MAP Q3 ▪ The Queenstown Story: Cobh Heritage Centre; 021 481 3591; open May–Oct: 9:30am–6pm Mon–Sat, 11am–6pm Sun; Nov–Apr: 9:30am–5pm Mon–Sat; adm

Pronounced "Cove", this 19th-century town boasts one of the world's largest natural harbours. In its heyday, the town was a major commercial seaport as well as being the stopover port for luxury passenger liners, including the *Sirius*, which made her maiden voyage from here. Cobh was also the last port of call for the *Titanic* before she sailed to her tragic end.

Blarney Castle, set in lush gardens

4 Blarney Castle
MAP Q3 ▪ Blarney ▪ 021 438 5252 ▪ Open daily ▪ Adm

It is really the Blarney Stone, believed to have been gifted to the King of Munster by Robert the Bruce, that brings visitors flocking here. Legend has it that whoever kisses the stone will be given the gift of eloquent speech. Now a partial ruin, the castle dates from the mid-15th century, and is surrounded by extensive grounds that feature an ice house, a poison garden filled with poisonous plants, and a bog garden with waterfalls.

5 Fota Wildlife Park
MAP Q3 ▪ Carrigtwohill, Cobh ▪ 021 481 2678 ▪ Open 10am–5pm Mon–Sat, 10:30am–5pm Sun ▪ Adm

This large centre located on Fota Island prides itself on breeding and reintroducing wild animals to their natural habitats. It also boasts a highly successful cheetah-breeding programme.

Fishing boats in Cobh harbour

6 Old Midleton Distillery
MAP Q3 ▪ Midleton ▪ 021 461 3594 ▪ Open daily ▪ Adm

Learn the story of Jameson Irish Whiskey via an excellent audiovisual presentation, a tasting and a tour of the still houses, a distiller's cottage and the mills and maltings.

Old Midleton Distillery

7 Royal Gunpowder Mills
MAP Q3 ▪ Ballincollig

Gunpowder was one of Cork's most important industries in the mid-19th century until the mills closed in 1903. Visitors can see the canals, sluices, mills and workers' cottages.

8 Kinsale
MAP Q3

The fact that Kinsale has its own gourmet food festival gives some idea of the calibre of restaurants and cafés here. It is probably the most prosperous and sophisticated fishing village in the country and, being only 27 km (17 miles) from Cork

CULTURAL CORK

Cork prides itself on its culture and is extremely proud of the Opera House, which offers a full programme of classical concerts, opera and ballet throughout the year. The Triskel Arts Centre is the venue for literary events, performance art and music. The high-profile annual jazz festival in October enjoys international status.

city, attracts locals and tourists in droves. The pretty harbour is the focal point and most of the activity centres on this area and the nearby backstreets.

9 Charles Fort
MAP Q3 ▪ Summer Cove, Kinsale ▪ 021 477 2263 ▪ Open Nov–mid-Mar: 10am–6pm daily; mid-Mar–Oct: 10am–6pm daily ▪ Adm

Built in the late 17th century, Charles Fort has been associated with some of the key events in Irish history, including the Williamite War (1689–91) and the Irish Civil War (1922–23).

10 Youghal
MAP Q4

About 50 km (31 miles) east of Cork city, Youghal (pronounced "yawl") has a great location on both the Atlantic Ocean and the River Blackwater's estuary. The walls enclosing the town were built by the English to protect the village from attack by the native Irish. Queen Elizabeth I bestowed Youghal on Sir Walter Raleigh. Under Cromwell, however, the town became an English Protestant garrison.

Picturesque Kinsale

Places to Eat

① Aherne's Seafood Restaurant and Bar
MAP Q4 ▪ 163 N Main St, Youghal ▪ 024 92424 ▪ €

This is a very popular, relaxed restaurant, serving delicious fresh seafood dishes, including a fantastic nine-course tasting menu.

② Blair's Inn
MAP Q3 ▪ Cloghroe, Blarney, Co Cork ▪ 021 438 1470 ▪ €

This award-winning bar-restaurant is full of nooks and crannies, with open fires in winter and a beer garden in summer. The speciality is local, seasonal fare: try O'Flynn's gourmet pork and leek sausages.

③ Longueville House
MAP Q3 ▪ Mallow, Co Cork ▪ 022 47156 ▪ €€

An elegant country-house hotel with delicious dining in rather grand surroundings. The owners produce their own apple brandy, garden berry liqueurs and cider, and coffee comes with handmade chocolates.

④ Ballymaloe House
MAP Q4 ▪ Shanagarry ▪ 021 465 2531 ▪ €€

Darina and Tim Allen's cookery school has a worldwide reputation and it is hardly surprising that the food is absolutely delicious.

⑤ Elbow Lane Brew and Smokehouse
MAP Q3 ▪ 4 Oliver Plunkett St, Cork ▪ 021 239 0479 ▪ €€

Set in a handsome town house, this "nanobrewery" specializes in delectable dishes from its own smokehouse, washed down with tasting trays of its home-made ales.

⑥ Isaacs
MAP Q3 ▪ 48 MacCurtain St, Cork ▪ 021 450 3805 ▪ Closed Sun lunch ▪ €€

Very popular with locals and visitors, this place serves award-winning food.

PRICE CATEGORIES
For a three-course meal for one with half a bottle of wine (or equivalent meal), taxes and extra charges.

€ under €45   €€ €45–€90   €€€ over €90

⑦ Café Paradiso
MAP Q3 ▪ 16 Lancaster Quay, Cork ▪ 021 427 7939 ▪ €€

This delightful restaurant, with wonderful staff, serves an elegant menu of inventive vegetarian cuisine made from quality ingredients.

Relaxed dining at Café Paradiso

⑧ Greenes
MAP Q3 ▪ 48 MacCurtain St, Cork ▪ 021 450 0011 ▪ €

A restaurant with its own waterfall sounds unlikely, but seeing is believing at this converted warehouse, whose picture windows look out onto a 60ft- (18m-) high cascade. The food doesn't disappoint, either.

⑨ An Súgán
MAP R3 ▪ 41 Wolf Tone St, Clonakilty ▪ 023 883 3719 ▪ €

The West Cork creamy chowder is a hit at this extremely popular restaurant and seafood bar.

⑩ Fishy Fishy Café
MAP Q3 ▪ Pier Rd, Kinsale ▪ 021 470 0415 ▪ €€

It's no surprise that fresh seafood is always on the menu at this bustling café beside Kinsale's pretty harbour.

See map on p94 ←

ᴛᴏᴘ10 Tipperary, Limerick and Clare

From the lush greenery of Tipperary to the traffic jams of Limerick, and from the pleasure boats cruising on the River Shannon to the stark emptiness of The Burren, this region embraces the full diversity of rural Ireland. There are scores of historic sights and picture-perfect villages, as well as unpretentious country towns with not a tourist in sight. Cross the Shannon to reach the rockier majesty of County Clare, whose rural way of life retains a profound simplicity. Culturally, it is rooted in tradition, and you'll hear plenty of Irish music played in village pubs. Clare's coastline rises in dramatic cliffs that take the force of the Atlantic, while inland, wind-battered gorse and bracken are broken up by high pasture.

The dramatic cliffs of Moher

① **Cliffs of Moher**
MAP N2 ▪ Visitors' Centre, Liscannor, Co Clare: open from 9am daily; 065 708 6141; adm
With five miles (8 km) of dramatic, sheer cliffs rising up as much as 702 ft (214 m) from the pounding Atlantic, this is definitely one of Europe's grandest stretches of coastline. Take the steep cliff-edge footpath round to O'Brien's Tower for some breathtaking views across the ocean.

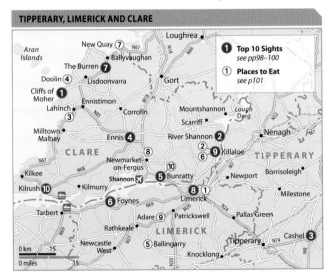

TIPPERARY, LIMERICK AND CLARE

> **1** Top 10 Sights
> see pp98–100
>
> ① Places to Eat
> see p101

Boats docked at Lough Derg

Ireland's earliest Romanesque church; the roofless 13th-century cathedral; and the 15th-century Vicars' Choral, the residential quarters of the cathedral cantors.

4 Ennis

MAP P3 ■ Friary: 065 682 9100; Open Apr–Sep: 10am–6pm Oct: 10am–5pm; adm

This likeable little town, with its bright shopfronts and music pubs, grew up in the 13th century around Ennis Friary. Shut down in 1692, the abbey fell into ruin but what survives – mostly 15th-century structures – includes the richly carved MacMahon Tomb.

2 River Shannon

MAP P2

Ireland's longest river opens into broad lakes, eventually widening into a huge estuary. The river's curve traditionally marks the border of the west. Lough Derg, the largest lake, is popular for boating and angling.

3 Cashel

MAP N2 ■ Cashel

This country town is dominated by the Rock of Cashel, topped by stone structures known in pre-Christian times as Cashel of Kings (from Gaelic *caiseal*, a stone fortress). Sensing the rising power of the church, in 1101 the Kings of Munster redefined themselves as a dynasty of royal archbishops and built great ecclesiastical buildings. Most were destroyed by the English in 1647, but highlights of what survives are the 12th-century Cormac's Chapel,

5 Bunratty Castle

MAP P3 ■ Bunratty ■ 061 360788 ■ Open 9:30am–5:30pm daily; last adm to castle 4pm ■ Adm

The sturdy 15th-century stronghold of the O'Briens, Earls of Thomond, has become a top venue for mock medieval banquets and other forms of entertainment. The five-storey structure was fully restored by Viscount Gort in 1954. Behind the castle, Bunratty Folk Park gives an insight into traditional rural culture.

6 Foynes Flying Boat Museum

MAP P2 ■ Foynes ■ Open mid-Mar–May: 9:30am–5pm; Jun–Sep: 9am–6pm ■ Adm

Transatlantic flights between Ireland and the US began in Foynes in 1939, and in 1942 the first nonstop passenger flights between Europe and America started here. The museum tells the story.

The impressive Rock of Cashel, with its ruined medieval buildings

King John's Castle and Hunt Museum, Limerick

7 The Burren

MAP N2 ▪ Burren Centre: Kilfenora; open Mar–May, Sep & Oct: 10am–5pm daily; Jun–Aug: 9:30am–5:30pm daily; 065 708 8030; adm

A weird limestone desert of flat rock "pavements", the 100-sq-mile (260-sq-km) Burren (pronounced "burn") seems mostly lifeless at first glance. But the web of hidden gulleys is brimming with plants, some very rare. Once densely populated, the Burren preserves dolmens, ruined towers and ring-forts. Visit the Burren Centre to learn more.

An ancient dolmen in the Burren

BURREN BOTANY

Apart from seasonal pools, called *turloughs*, the Burren's limestone does not hold water. Yet more than 1,100 plant species thrive here, because countless cracks in the rocks and stones accumulate organic matter and provide shelter. Especially common are mosses, lichens, rock rose, mountain avens, orchids and bloody cranesbill.

8 Limerick

MAP P3 ▪ King John's Castle: open Apr–Sep: 9:30am–5:30pm daily; Oct–Nov: 9:30am–5pm daily; adm ▪ Hunt Museum: Rutland St; open 10am–5pm Mon–Sat, 2–5pm Sun; adm

A grim portrait of industrial Limerick, the third-largest city in the republic, was painted by Frank McCourt's novel *Angela's Ashes (see p43)*. It's not that bad now. The city centre has good restaurants and pubs and a pleasant atmosphere. Historical sights include the imposing King John's Castle. Built in 1210, the castle is home to the excellent Hunt Museum, with its magnificent collection of Irish antiquities.

9 Killaloe

MAP P3

A chic marina town rising steeply from the southern end of Lough Derg and a centre for water sports. The 12th-century St Flannan's Cathedral and Oratory have fine Romanesque decorative stonework.

10 Kilrush and Loop Head Drive

MAP P2 ▪ Kilrush Heritage Centre: open Apr–Sep: 10am–5pm Mon–Fri, 1–5pm Sun; Oct–Mar: 10am–4pm Mon–Fri; adm

While Kilrush itself is unremarkable, it makes a good base for exploring the furthest reaches of southwest County Clare. Especially worthwhile is a drive out to Loop Head. For an insight into local history, particularly the hardships under English rule, visit the Kilrush Heritage Centre.

See map on p98

Places to Eat

Copper and Spice
MAP P3 ■ Annacotty Village, Limerick ■ 061 338791 ■ €

A stylish restaurant that presents Indian-Asian cuisine, with lots of good options for vegetarians. There is a take-away menu too.

Cherry Tree Restaurant
MAP P3 ■ Lakeside, Ballina Killaloe ■ 061 375688 ■ €€

Thanks to its consistently good cooking and pretty Shannon-side views, this is a County Clare favourite. Typical dishes include fillet of beef, Bluebell Falls goat's cheese and slow-roasted pork belly.

Barrtra Seafood Restaurant
MAP N2 ■ Miltown Malbay Rd, Lahinch, Co Clare ■ 065 708 1280 ■ Opening times vary ■ €€

This cliff-side, bay-facing cottage is an institution, offering a kind welcome and wonderful seafood.

Cullinans
MAP N2 ■ Doolin ■ 065 707 4183 ■ Open Easter–Oct ■ €

A family-owned restaurant (and guesthouse) in the centre of Doolin village, Cullinans is renowned for its locally caught fresh seafood.

The Mustard Seed
MAP P3 ■ Echo Lodge, Ballingarry ■ 069 68508 ■ €€

Set within a Victorian country-house hotel, this bustling, stylish restaurant offers fine modern Irish cuisine as well as an excellent wine list.

PRICE CATEGORIES
For a three-course meal for one with half a bottle of wine (or equivalent meal), taxes and extra charges.

€ under €45 €€ €45–€90 €€€ over €90

Molly's Bar and Restaurant
MAP P3 ■ Ballina, Killaloe ■ 061 376 632 ■ €

A pub-style restaurant on the shores of Lough Derg, Molly's serves simply cooked, fresh, local produce.

Linnane's Lobster Bar
MAP N2 ■ The Pier, New Quay ■ 065 707 8120 ■ €

Stunning views of the Burren and Aughinish Island complement the delicious seafood on offer here.

Earl of Thomond
MAP P3 ■ Newmarket-on-Fergus ■ 061 368144 ■ €€

Dromoland Castle is the perfect place for a lunch or dinner after a day on the adjoining golf course.

The Arches
MAP P3 ■ Main St, Adare ■ 061 396246 ■ €

This family-run eatery in the centre of one of Ireland's prettiest villages has a diverse international menu.

Durty Nelly's Oyster Restaurant
MAP P3 ■ Bunratty ■ 061 364861 ■ €

This mellow village inn, in the shadow of Bunratty Castle, has been in business since 1620.

Durty Nelly's Oyster Restaurant

Clonmacnoise and the Midlands

1 Belvedere House

MAP N4 ■ N52, Mullingar ■ 044 394 9060 ■ Open Jan, Feb, Nov & Dec: 9:30am–4:30pm daily; Mar–Sep: 9:30am–6pm daily ■ Adm

There was no sense or sensibility in the actions of the Earl of Belvedere, despite the Austen-style setting of his house. He began the house in 1740, spent his life fighting his brothers and built the Gothic Jealous Wall to block the view of his sibling's house. He also locked up his wife for 31 years, suspecting she'd slept with one of them.

Elegant interiors at Belvedere House

2 Tullynally Castle

MAP M4 ■ Castlepollard ■ 044 966 1159 ■ Castle: open to groups by arrangement; Gardens: open Apr–Oct: 11am–6pm Thu–Sun; adm

Constructed in the 17th century, most of Tullynally today is a result of the second Earl of Longford's remodelling of it as a Gothic Revival castle, housing a collection of Irish furniture and portraits. Outside are romantic grounds.

3 Emo Court

MAP N4 ■ Portlaoise ■ 057 862 6573 ■ House: open Easter–Sep: 10am–6pm daily; Gardens: open dawn–dusk daily; adm to house

Designed in 1790 for the Earl of Portarlington, this is another fine example of architect James Gandon's work, and his interiors in this lovely house remain unchanged. The gardens are divided into two sections: the Grapery leads you down to a lakeside walk; the Clucker acquired its name from the nuns who used to reside here.

4 The Kilbeggan Distillery Experience

MAP N4 ■ Kilbeggan, Co Westmeath ■ 057 933 2134 ■ Open Apr–Oct: 9am–6pm daily; Nov–Mar: 10am–4pm daily; last adm 1 hr before closing ■ Adm ■ www.kilbeggandistillery.com

Originally known as Locke's, the distillery closed in 1957, a full two centuries after getting its licence in 1757. It has now been restored as a museum, displaying original 1920s machinery and offering an intriguing glimpse into the lives of the people who worked there. Visitors receive a complimentary sample of Kilbeggan Irish Whiskey at the end of the guided (or self-guided) tour.

5 Clonmacnoise

MAP N4 ■ Shannonbridge ■ 0909 674195 ■ Open mid-Mar–May, Sep & Oct: 10am–6pm daily; Jun–Aug: 9am–6:30pm daily; Nov–mid-Mar: 10am–5:30pm daily ■ Adm

This early Christian site, founded by St Ciaran in the 6th century, draws tourists into Ireland's often neglected Midlands. The grounds are atmospheric, especially on a grey Irish day, and include the ruins of a cathedral, seven churches (10th–13th centuries), two round towers, three high crosses and dozens of early Christian grave slabs. The visitors' centre offers an audiovisual history of the site and various exhibitions.

Celtic Cross at Clonmacnoise

Impressive Birr Castle, dating back to medieval times

6 Birr Castle, Gardens and Science Centre

MAP N4 ▪ Birr ▪ 057 912 0336 ▪ Open mid-Mar–Oct: 9am–6pm daily; Nov–mid-Mar: 10am–4pm daily ▪ Adm

The award-winning gardens are the highlight here, with 2,000 species of rare trees, shrubs and flowers and wonderful wildlife, as well as a lake and waterfalls. Birr's grounds also host a Science Centre, featuring the third Earl of Rosse's 1840s telescope, which for decades was the largest in the world. The earl's discovery of spiralling galaxies is brought to life by the centre's interactive exhibits.

7 Birr
MAP N4

Although dominated by the castle and its grounds, the town of Birr has much to offer visitors. Its beautiful Georgian buildings have been lovingly preserved, with many houses retaining their original fanlights and door panelling.

8 Slieve Bloom Mountains
MAP N4

Despite only rising 527 m (1,729 ft), the surrounding flat plain aids in creating an imposing image of the Slieve Bloom Mountains, a National Nature Reserve. The Slieve Bloom Way has been marked out for hikers.

9 Bog of Allen
MAP N5 ▪ Bog of Allen Nature Centre, Lullymore: 045 860133; open 9am–5pm Mon–Fri

Once the largest raised peat bog in Ireland, the Bog of Allen has been gradually shrinking after many centuries of agricultural exploitation. It is home to some of Ireland's most interesting indigenous plants and insects, including the carnivorous sundew and Venus Fly Trap.

10 Rock of Dunamase
MAP N4 ▪ Laois

Towering 45 m (150 ft) above a flat plain, the Rock of Dunamase, with its castle ruins, is one of the most impressive and historic sights in Ireland. The sight was included on Ptolemy's world map in AD 140, such was its fame, and the ruins date back thousands of years. Standing here, you can see all the way to the Slieve Bloom Mountains.

The ruins of Dunamase Castle

🔟 Around Galway

County Galway has a peculiar majesty and a sense of its closeness to nature, stalwartly facing the Atlantic Ocean. Even the area around the county town, Galway City, squeezed onto a strip of land between the expanse of Lough Corrib and the immense waters of Galway Bay, possesses that same inspiring quality. With its fine restaurants and charming pubs, Galway is a good base from which to explore the area. South of the city is a gentler, greener countryside. While a good deal of the fascination of this southern edge of Galway lies simply in the landscape, for lovers of literature much of the interest is also in the connection with the romantic Irish poet W B Yeats. Although not originally from this region, Yeats spent many years living at Thoor Ballylee near Gort.

The Claddagh, an old fishing village near Galway city centre

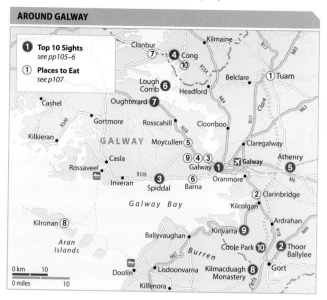

AROUND GALWAY

1 **Top 10 Sights**
see pp105–6

1 **Places to Eat**
see p107

1 Galway City
MAP N3

The pleasant, bustling regional capital started life as a fortress of the O'Connors of Connacht. Colonized in 1235 by Anglo-Normans, it became a prosperous seaport: some fine buildings survive, notably 16th-century Lynch's Castle (now a bank), and 14th-century St Nicholas's Church. There's a great atmosphere, with plenty of music and traditional shops.

The crumbling ruins of Athenry Dominican priory

2 Thoor Ballylee
MAP N3 ▪ Gort ▪ 091 537700 ▪ Open 10am–2pm Mon–Fri, 11am–5pm Sat & Sun (Jun–Aug: 10am–6pm daily) ▪ Adm ▪ www.yeatsthoor ballylee.org

The old tower house in which W B Yeats and his wife Georgie spent much time during the 1920s is a sturdy little fortress. Restored and converted by Yeats, it is described with touching detail in many of his poems.

3 Spiddal
MAP N2

Officially Irish-speaking, and hosting a Gaelic summer school, Spiddal makes a pleasant stop on the Galway Bay coast road. Several craft workers have set up shop in the Spiddal Craft Village, where you can see pottery, weaving, knitting and other skilled work in progress, and of course buy the beautiful finished goods.

4 Cong Abbey
MAP M2 ▪ Cong

Poised on the narrow strip between Lough Corrib and Lough Mask, the attractive village of Cong lies just across the Galway border in County Mayo. Cong Abbey was an important Augustinian community founded by the King of Connacht in 1120. Closed down during the Reformation, it fell into ruin. What survives, including the lovely cloisters, remains majestic.

5 Athenry
MAP N3

The poignant folksong "The Fields of Athenry" (pronounced "athen-rye") gives little clue about this evocative reminder of the Anglo-Norman colonists. In 1235, Meyler de Bermingham was granted a charter to Athenry, where he built a little castle and founded a Dominican Priory in 1241 where he and his descendants could be buried. Today, though damaged, much survives, together with a broken 15th-century cross erected in the central square.

6 Lough Corrib
MAP N2

The vast expanse of Lough Corrib's cool waters, feeling more like part of the Atlantic Ocean, is Ireland's second largest lake, and a popular resort area for angling, various water sports and walking.

Serene and idyllic Lough Corrib

TO BE CARVED

One of W B Yeats's poems is entitled *To Be Carved on a Stone at Thoor Ballylee*, and the words have indeed been carved at Yeats's old tower house: "I, the poet William Yeats, / With old mill boards and sea-green slates, / And smithy work from the Gort forge, / Restored this tower for my wife George; / And may these characteristics remain / When all is ruin once again."

Boats at Kinvara's fishing harbour

7 Oughterard
MAP N2 ▪ Aughnanure Castle: open Apr–Oct: 9:30am–6pm daily; adm

Located on the shores of Lough Corrib, this village has become a small resort area. Its chief prize, however, is Aughnanure Castle; set beside the lake, this is a handsome remnant of a 16th-century tower house of the O'Flaherty clan of Connacht, who terrorized the ruling Anglo-Norman families of Galway.

8 Kilmacduagh Monastery
MAP N3 ▪ Gort

An astonishing set of monastic abbey ruins survives here. The original church, established in 610, was enlarged over the centuries and replaced by a cathedral in the 11th or 12th century, though keeping many features of the older buildings, including an 11th-century door. Around it are other intriguing 13th- and 14th-century ecclesiastical buildings. There's even a "Leaning Tower", built in the 10th century.

Kilmacduagh Monastery

9 Kinvara
MAP N3

The little road around Galway Bay passes through a score of villages that are breathtaking in their prettiness and grandiose location. The most charming is Kinvara, with its fishing harbour and pier cottages. It's the setting for a traditional music festival in May, and a Gathering of the Boats festival in August.

10 Coole Park
MAP N3 ▪ Gort ▪ Open summer: 8am–7:30pm daily; winter: 8am–6pm daily ▪ www.coolepark.ie

The woods, lakes and paths of this national park and wildlife reserve, with its red deer, were once the grounds of a great Georgian mansion, home of Lady Augusta Gregory. Augusta hosted the most famous novelists and playwrights of her day and the Irish Revival began here.

Places to Eat

1 Cre na Cille

MAP M3 ■ High St, Tuam ■ 093 28232 ■ Open Tue–Sat ■ €€

Seafood, meat and game are the specialities of this excellent, unassuming family-run restaurant. It also has a large array of fine whiskeys.

2 Paddy Burke's Oyster Inn

MAP N3 ■ Clarinbridge ■ 091 796226 ■ €

The best time to visit this pub is during Clarinbridge's September oyster festival. As well as shellfish from the famed local beds, it offers a choice of good meat and fish dishes.

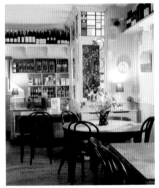

Ard Bia at Nimmos

3 Ard Bia at Nimmos

MAP N3 ■ Spanish Arch, Galway City ■ 091 561114 ■ €

Restaurant, café, art gallery – this reputable eatery offers a delicious menu with Irish, European and Middle Eastern influences. Try Colleran's spiced lamb *borek*.

4 The Seafood Bar @ Kirwan's Lane

MAP N3 ■ Kirwan's Lane, Galway City ■ 091 568266 ■ €€

A pretty restaurant serving creative cuisine with a modern Irish theme, such as linguine with fresh clams and langoustines.

PRICE CATEGORIES

For a three-course meal for one with half a bottle of wine (or equivalent meal), taxes and extra charges.

€ under €45 €€ €45–€90 €€€ over €90

5 White Gables

MAP N2 ■ Moycullen Village ■ 091 555744 ■ €€

Set in an informal whitewashed 19th-century inn, White Gables is best known for its lobster, but also serves other "surf and turf" dishes.

6 Pins Gastro Bar

MAP N2 ■ The Twelve Hotel, Barna Village, Galway ■ 091 597000 ■ €

The emphasis is on top-quality locally sourced produce at this restaurant serving modern Irish food.

7 Burke's Bar and Restaurant

MAP N3 ■ Mount Gable House, Clonbur, Co Galway ■ 094 954 6175 ■ €

This pub in the village of Clonbur serves meat, fish and poultry dishes as well as home-baked scones.

8 Aran Islands Hotel

MAP N2 ■ Kilronan, Inis Mór, Aran Islands ■ 099 61104 ■ €

Modern Irish cuisine is served in the cosy surroundings of the restaurant and bar at this island hotel overlooking Kilronan Harbour.

9 McDonagh's Seafood House

MAP N3 ■ 22 Quay St, Galway City ■ 091 565001 ■ €

As you might expect, this place specializes in fresh seafood.

10 Hungry Monk Café

MAP M2 ■ Abbey St, Cong, Co Mayo ■ 094 954 5842 ■ €

Enjoy a lunch or gourmet snack at this down-to-earth village café. The home-made baking and desserts alone are worth stopping for.

See map on p104

🔟 Connemara and Mayo

Connemara – the rocky, mountainous countryside of western County Galway – is largely uncultivated, a strange wilderness of water and stone, peat bog, headlands and barren hills. Along its shores, the Atlantic eats into the land, making spectacular inlets and bays. Thousands of rough dry-stone walls criss-cross the bare hills, enclosing tiny abandoned fields. The famine wiped out most of Connemara's population, and the memory of that disaster lingers in the glorious landscape. Across Killary Fjord and into County Mayo, you'll find appealing small towns and a traditional way of life, as well as wide open spaces of bog, heath, mountain and lake.

The Sky Road with its scenic views

① Sky Road
MAP M1

Named for its beautiful cliff-edge ocean views, the Sky Road is a 11-km (7-mile) loop that starts out from Clifden and skirts the narrow peninsula alongside Clifden Bay. Along the way you'll see empty beaches, fabulous wild hill scenery, and sights such as the ruins of Neo-Gothic Clifden Castle, the home of Clifden's founder John d'Arcy.

CONNEMARA AND MAYO

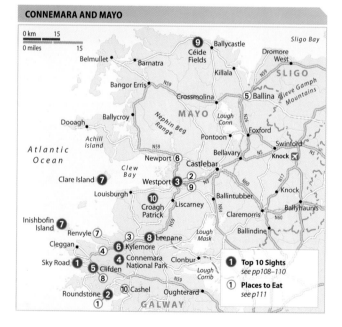

① **Top 10 Sights**
see pp108–110

① **Places to Eat**
see p111

Picturesque Roundstone harbour, with its lobster-fishing boats

2 Roundstone
MAP N2

Cloch na Rón is the official name of this attractively laid out, Irish-speaking "planned village" built in the 1820s. It's an authentic, unpretentious lobster-fishing community, but it also has an arty side and many attractions for visitors, including a good beach, galleries and traditional shops.

3 Westport
MAP M2 ▪ Westport House: open Mar–Oct: times vary; adm

Busy, popular Westport is still small enough that countryside can be seen at the end of the main streets. Originally built in 1780 by the Earl of Altamont as an adjunct to his mansion, Westport House, this is a good example of a planned town, with its dignified central Octagon and tree-lined Mall. It was all paid for by the slave-worked West Indian sugar plantations of the Earl's wife. Westport House remains imposing and grandly furnished, with a number of attractions such as a pirate adventure park for children.

4 Connemara National Park and Twelve Bens Mountains
MAP M2 ▪ Visitors' Centre: Letterfrack; 095 41054; open 9am–5:30pm daily

Extending from Letterfrack village to the Twelve Bens, this national park is a lovely 30-sq-km (11-sq-mile) conservation area of heath, bog and hills encompassing the grandest of Connemara's landscapes. The Twelve Bens, a dozen high peaks rising from the heart of the western mountains, dominate Connemara's skyline. A visitors' centre near the park entrance has a permanent exhibition on the flora, fauna, geology and history of the region.

Sheep in Connemara National Park

5 Clifden
MAP M1

Regarded as the "capital" of Connemara, although hardly more than a village, this busy little resort lies among lovely green hills above Clifden Bay and at the foot of the Twelve Bens Mountains. A Georgian planned town built by John d'Arcy, it retains a certain character and style. At the end of summer, Clifden hosts the Connemara Pony Show, which brings in hordes of horse-lovers.

The beautifully sited Kylemore Abbey, next to Kylemore Lough

⑥ Kylemore Abbey
MAP M2 ▪ Kylemore ▪ 095 52001 ▪ Open daylight hours daily ▪ Adm

The extraordinarily over-elaborate mock-Gothic castle, built in 1868 for millionaire Mitchell Henry, has been a Benedictine convent since the 1920s. Although a religious community, it is also run as a commercial tourist attraction. The house and walled gardens are delightful and their location magnificent, next to Kylemore Lough and with views towards the Twelve Bens.

⑦ Clare and Inishbofin Islands
MAP M1

Dramatic Clare Island was the stronghold of Grace O'Malley, or Granuaile, whose little fortress still stands, as does the ruined abbey where she is buried. Inishbofin has a green, lonely beauty. Home of the O'Flaherty clan and a hideaway of Grace O'Malley, it was taken by Cromwell. Both islands have small populations and prehistoric ruins.

⑧ Leenane to Killary Harbour
MAP M2

The appealing village of Leenane lies beside the long, narrow inlet of Killary Fjord. From here, the dramatically beautiful road to the small oceanside resort of Louisburgh crosses the water between the peaks of Devil's Mother and Ben Gorm, and rises among lakes and streams along the narrow Delphi Valley.

⑨ Céide Fields
MAP L2 ▪ Open Apr–May & Oct: 10am–5pm daily; Jun–Sep: 10am–6pm daily ▪ Adm

Preserved for thousands of years under a blanket of peat bog, the Céide site consists of Stone Age walled fields, together with stone ruins. Excellent guided tours are offered by the visitors' centre.

⑩ Croagh Patrick
MAP M2

This is one of the most sacred sites in Ireland. St Patrick fasted on the summit for 40 days in AD 441. It is considered a pious act to make the steep climb to the summit.

Pilgrims ascending Croagh Patrick

GRACE O'MALLEY

Grace O'Malley (1530–1603) was the daughter of a Connacht chieftain. At 15, she married the O'Flaherty chief, whose men remained loyal to her after his death. With fortresses throughout Connacht, and based on Clare Island, she visited Queen Elizabeth I in 1593, extracting a promise to be left in peace.

Places to Eat

PRICE CATEGORIES
For a three-course meal for one with half a bottle of wine (or equivalent meal), taxes and extra charges.

€ under €45   €€ €45–€90   €€€ over €90

1 O'Dowd's Seafood Bar and Restaurant
MAP N2 ▪ Roundstone ▪ 095 35809 ▪ €

Beside Roundstone's pretty harbour, O'Dowd's serves steak and seafood dishes and caters more for vegetarians than most Irish restaurants.

2 La Fougère

MAP M2 ▪ Knockranny House Hotel, Westport, Co Mayo ▪ 098 28600 ▪ €€

This multi-award-winning restaurant is set on a hill a short walk from the town centre. It offers stunning views of the water and delicious fare.

3 Kylemore Abbey
MAP M2 ▪ Kylemore Abbey, Connemara, Co Galway ▪ 095 52001 ▪ €

Irish stew and beef-and-Guinness casserole, with ingredients from the Abbey's garden, are some of the traditional dishes on offer.

4 Rosleague Manor
MAP M2 ▪ Letterfrack ▪ 095 41101 ▪ Open to non-residents by reservation ▪ €

Connemara lamb and local seafood are specialities of the house, served with the best local ingredients.

5 Crockets on the Quay
MAP L2 ▪ Ballina ▪ 096 75930 ▪ €

An affordable, friendly and relaxed restaurant and bar on the quay, serving modern Irish cuisine.

6 Newport House
MAP M2 ▪ Newport ▪ 098 41222 ▪ €€

Set in a lovely Georgian mansion, this restaurant bases its menu on fresh produce from its own farm, gardens and fishery, and smokes its own salmon. What's more, it boasts a superb wine cellar.

7 Renvyle House
MAP M1 ▪ Renvyle ▪ 095 46100 ▪ €

A gracious country-house hotel on the shores of the Atlantic serving superb seafood, Connemara lamb and other classic Irish and European dishes. Booking is strongly recommended.

8 Mitchell's
MAP M1 ▪ Market St, Clifden, Co Galway ▪ 095 21867 ▪ €

An excellent family-style restaurant in the Connemara village of Clifden, serving comforting, home-style food, such as seafood and poultry dishes, in a relaxed setting.

The cosy interior of JW's Brasserie

9 JW's Brasserie

MAP M2 ▪ The Octagon, Westport, Co Mayo ▪ 098 25027 ▪ €

Housed in the Wyatt Hotel, this award-winning contemporary Irish restaurant is popular with locals and tourists alike.

10 Cashel House
MAP N2 ▪ Cashel ▪ 095 31001 ▪ €€

Previously a gracious aristocratic home, this country house and restaurant has now earned itself international renown for both its food and atmosphere.

See map on p108

🔟 Yeats Country and the Northwest

The Northwest incorporates some of Ireland's finest and most dramatic scenery, with its beautiful wide sandy beaches, towering mountains, woodland and forest parks. Driving is the best way to tour this part of the country as public transport is all but non-existent. The region's colloquial name is in honour of the two great Irish brothers, Jack B and W B Yeats, artist and poet respectively, who spent much of their boyhood in the ancient Celtic town of Sligo. This was also the legendary power base of the warrior Queen Maeve of Connaught and is packed with prehistoric sites. Donegal was left somewhat isolated when it was excluded from the new Northern Ireland in 1921 and has little in common with its fellow counties.

Mount Errigal, Glenveagh National Park

YEATS COUNTRY AND THE NORTHWEST

1 Top 10 Sights
see pp113–14

1 Places to Eat
see p115

1 Glenveagh National Park
MAP K4 ▪ Co Donegal
▪ 076 100 2537 ▪ Open Mar–Oct:
9am–5:30pm daily; Nov–Feb:
9am–5pm daily

The extraordinary quartzite cone of Mount Errigal dominates the Derryveagh mountain range in this wild part of Donegal. It overlooks the Glenveagh National Park, which incorporates the beautiful Lough Veagh Valley, and Poison Glen.

2 Sligo
MAP L3 ▪ Co Sligo

This busy market town is home to the excellent Model Arts Centre and Niland Gallery, which has a collection of Jack B Yeats's paintings, as well as quirky, arty shops, good bookshops and fine restaurants. To the east of town is the lovely Lough Gill, which has a number of woodland walks, while brooding Benbulben Mountain and the fine sandy beaches of Strandhill and Rosses Point are only a 10-minute drive away.

3 Inishowen Peninsula
MAP K4 ▪ Co Donegal

Undiscovered by so many, this glorious corner in the far northwest has possibly the finest scenery in Ireland, with the spectacular Slieve Snaght Mountain in the centre, Foyle and Swilly lakes to the east and west, and the dune-fringed beaches facing the Atlantic. The peninsula also has its share of dramatic headlands and boasts Ireland's most northwesterly point at rugged Malin Head.

Drumcliffe church, built in 1809

4 Lissadell and Drumcliffe
MAP L3 ▪ Ballinfull, Co Sligo
▪ Lissadell House: www.lissadell.com

North of Sligo is Drumcliffe church, where W B Yeats (see p42) is buried; the visitors' centre focuses on items and books relating to the poet. Yeats was a frequent visitor at nearby Lissadell House, home to the Gore-Booth family, who were active in the fight for Irish freedom.

5 Parke's Castle
MAP L3 ▪ Fivemile Bourne, Co Leitrim ▪ 071 916 4149 ▪ Open Apr–Sep: 10am–6pm daily ▪ Adm

Overlooking Lough Gill, this moated, fortified manor house, accessible by road or boat, was erected on the site of an earlier house. Much of the earlier structure is incorporated into the castle, but otherwise it is a fine example of a Plantation house.

Five-Finger Strand at Malin Head

Castle Island, with its romantic folly castle, on Lough Key

6 Lough Key and Boyle
MAP M3 ■ Co Roscommon

One of the best spots for viewing this magnificent lake is from the main Sligo-to-Boyle road. The Lough Key Forest Park has numerous walks along the lakeside and through the woods. Nearby is the appealing town of Boyle, with a ruined abbey, interesting museum and some very fine Georgian architecture.

7 Slieve League
MAP L3 ■ Co Donegal ■ Slieve League Cliffs Centre: www.slieve leaguecliffs.ie

Europe's highest accessible sea cliffs plunge some 1,970 ft (600 m) into the Atlantic – that's almost three times higher than the more famous Cliffs of Moher *(see p98)*. The viewing platform can be reached via a precipitous 4-mile (6-km) drive from Teelin village, passing the Slieve League Cliffs Centre, with its café, craft shop and art gallery, on the way.

8 Donegal
MAP L4 ■ Co Donegal

Donegal is most famous for its tweed production, with Magee of Donegal the biggest manufacturer based here. The Diamond, a triangular central market, is at the heart of the town and an obelisk in the centre commemorates the four Gaelic Franciscans who wrote *The Annals of the Four Masters* in the 1630s. This extraordinary opus follows the history of the Gaelic people from the Great Flood up to the 17th century.

THE GAELTACHTS

The area around Donegal is one of the largest Gaelic-speaking *(Gaeltacht)* regions of the country. Until the 17th century most of the Irish population spoke Gaelic, the only other language being Latin. During British rule, use of the language diminished as English took over, but it is steadily reviving.

9 Letterkenny
MAP K4 ■ Co Donegal

County Donegal's largest town is flanked to the west by the Derryveagh Mountains and the Sperrin Mountains to the east. Visit the Gothic St Eunan's Cathedral and the County Museum.

10 Horn Head
MAP K4 ■ Co Donegal

This dramatic 600-ft (180-m) rock face, with stupendous views over the Atlantic, is home to hundreds of seabirds, including gulls and puffins.

The dramatic cliffs of Horn Head

Places to Eat

1 Eithna's by the Sea
MAP L3 ■ The Harbour, Mullaghmore, Co Sligo ■ 071 916 6407 ■ €€

At this bracing, long-established harbourside spot in Mullaghmore, the owner Eithna O'Sullivan does wonders with lobster, hake, clams and mussels – her seaweed pesto is so good they sell it in jars. Try to get a table outdoors.

2 Rathmullan House
MAP K4 ■ Rathmullan, Co Donegal ■ 074 915 8188 ■ €€

Gourmet dinners are made with locally sourced ingredients, many from the walled organic garden, and are served in the Pavilion room at this grand country-house hotel.

Oysters at Kealy's Seafood Bar

3 Kealy's Seafood Bar
MAP K5 ■ Greencastle, Co Donegal ■ 074 938 1010 ■ €

Located beside the pier, this atmospheric restaurant-bar serves first-class seafood and a range of meat and vegetarian dishes. There's traditional Irish music most Sundays.

4 The Mill Restaurant
MAP K4 ■ Dunfanaghy, Co Donegal ■ 074 913 6985 ■ €€

An old flax mill has been converted into a family-run restaurant, which offers tasty roasts and seafood dishes accompanied by local craft beers and a selection of wines. It also offers B&B accommodation.

PRICE CATEGORIES
For a three-course meal for one with half a bottle of wine (or equivalent meal), taxes and extra charges.

€ under €45   €€ €45–€90   €€€ over €90

5 Woodhill House
MAP K3 ■ Ardara, Co Donegal ■ 074 954 1112 ■ €€

This coastal manor house has an excellent French-style restaurant. Try the fresh seafood landed at the nearby fishing village of Killybegs.

6 Coach Lane Restaurant
MAP L3 ■ 1–2 Lord Edward St, Sligo ■ 071 916 2417 ■ €€

Sample a delicious variety of cooking styles and dishes, such as Clew Bay scallops, free-range poussin and local Lissadell mussels and clams.

7 Yeats Tavern
MAP L3 ■ Drumcliffe, Co Sligo ■ 071 916 3117 ■ €

This large, modern restaurant is a popular stopping place on the way to Donegal. The helpings are generous and there's a huge choice.

8 Montmartre
MAP L3 ■ 1 Market Yard, Sligo, Co Sligo ■ 071 916 9901 ■ €€

The creative menus here feature authentic French and European cuisine, and the wine list is excellent.

9 Fiddlers Creek
MAP L3 ■ Rockwood Parade, Sligo, Co Sligo ■ 071 914 1866 ■ €

A popular pub and restaurant on the Garavogue River, Fiddlers Creek serves tasty seafood, meat and poultry dishes.

10 Smuggler's Creek Inn
MAP L3 ■ Rossnowlagh, Co Donegal ■ 071 985 2366 ■ €

Take a table with a view in this family-run restaurant overlooking the sweep of Donegal Bay.

See map on p112

🔟 Northern Ireland

Northern Ireland remained under UK administration when the rest of Ireland became independent in 1921. A distinctive society has developed here, rooted in the historic cultural divide between Nationalists (Catholics of Irish descent) and Loyalists (Protestants of English and Scottish descent). Yet between Northern Ireland and the Republic there are more similarities than differences, from music to food and drink. The region has some of the most stunning landscapes in the country.

The extraordinary rock formations at the Giant's Causeway

NORTHERN IRELAND

① **Top 10 Sights**
see pp117–18

① **Places to Eat**
see p119

St Patrick's Cathedral, Armagh

1 Castle Ward
MAP L6 ■ Strangford, Co Down
■ 028 448 81204 ■ House: open Mar–Oct (times vary); Grounds: open all year ■ Adm

Strikingly set beside Strangford Lough, this 18th-century mansion has been home to the Ward family since 1570. There are numerous walking and cycling trails in the landscaped grounds. Also sited in the grounds, the estate's Clearsky Adventure Centre offers archery beside the medieval tower house, which starred as "Winterfell" in the drama series *Game of Thrones*.

2 Giant's Causeway
MAP K5 ■ Bushmills, Co Antrim
■ 028 2073 1855

The Giant's Causeway, designated a World Heritage Site since 1986, is a truly remarkable natural spectacle, its thousands of extraordinary hexagonal pillars of basalt rock clustered like a gigantic piece of honeycomb. The rocks descend from seafront cliffs into the water and disappear from view. Supposedly created by legendary warrior Fionn mac Cumhaill (*see p41*) as his stepping stones to Scotland, the Causeway was really created by a volcanic eruption some 60 million years ago.

3 Belfast
MAP L6 ■ Belfast Welcome Centre: 9 Donegall Sq N; open daily

Northern Ireland's capital is a vibrant Victorian city with shops, pubs, museums and galleries. Call at the Belfast Welcome Centre for details of the city's attractions, such as the absorbing Titanic Belfast museum.

4 Armagh
MAP L5

The city where Queen Macha built her fortress some 3,000 years ago, Armagh has a curious role in Ulster's religious divide. St Patrick based himself here, and the city is considered the ecclesiastical capital of both communities, with both a Catholic and a Protestant cathedral.

5 Glens of Antrim
MAP K5

Among the finest scenery in Ireland is the coast of County Antrim, where nine beautiful valleys (glens) cut deeply through high rolling hills to descend grandly into the sea. Follow the A2 through Carnlough, with its harbour, through Waterfoot, with waterfalls and a Forest Park, all the way up to the Giant's Causeway.

6 Lower Lough Erne
MAP L4

The serene waters and small islands extending north from Enniskillen can be explored by boat, or toured by road. Devenish Island is the remarkable site of 6th-century monastic ruins, a Celtic High Cross and a 30-m (100-ft) Round Tower.

The Titanic Belfast

The enchanting Italian Garden at Mount Stewart House

7 Ulster-American Folk Park

MAP L4 ■ Near Omagh ■ Open Mar–Sep: 10am–5pm Tue–Sun; Oct–Feb: 10am–4pm Tue–Fri, 11am–4pm Sat & Sun ■ Adm

This fascinating open-air museum reconstructs the lives of Irish emigrants on both sides of the Atlantic, and contains more than 30 historic buildings, churches, settler homesteads and even an emigrant ship.

Period furnishings at Florence Court

8 Florence Court

MAP L4 ■ A32, near Enniskillen ■ Opening hours vary; see the website (www.nationaltrust.org) for more information

The grandiose 18th-century Palladian Florence Court mansion originally belonged to the Earls of Enniskillen. Among the original features are an ice house and a water-driven sawmill.

9 Mount Stewart House

MAP L6 ■ Strangford Lough, near Newtownards ■ 028 4278 8387 ■ Lakeside Gardens: open 10am–5pm daily; House and Formal Gardens: open mid-Mar–Oct: 11am–5pm daily ■ Adm

The grandly aristocratic 18th-century Neo-Classical home of the Marquess of Londonderry displays a superb art collection, and stands in wonderful landscaped gardens with remarkable plant collections. There are some exquisite planned views, extraordinary topiary, and many odd stone-carvings representing creatures such as dodos and dinosaurs.

10 Derry (Londonderry)

MAP K4

At the heart of Derry (Londonderry), is a fascinating walled Plantation town, its 400-year-old fortifications almost intact. Free Derry Corner contains the famous political mural "You Are Now Entering Free Derry", which was painted in 1969.

THE SIX COUNTIES

The nine counties of the Kingdom of Ulster were the last part of Ireland to be subdued by the English. The kingdom's conquest in 1607 led to an exodus of Irish nobility, whose lands were "planted" with British Protestants. When the War of Independence created the Republic of Ireland, six of the Ulster counties remained British under the name of Northern Ireland.

Places to Eat

PRICE CATEGORIES

For a three-course meal for one with half a bottle of wine (or equivalent meal), taxes and extra charges.

£ under £35   ££ £35–£55   £££ over £55

 The Portaferry Hotel
MAP L6 ▪ The Strand, Portaferry ▪ 028 4272 8231 ▪ £

This restaurant on the shores of Strangford Lough has a high reputation for top-quality shellfish and other seafood, most of it fresh from the waters of the lake.

2 OX
MAP L6 ▪ 1 Oxford St, Belfast ▪ 028 9031 412 ▪ £££

Offering a menu that is centred around local and seasonal produce, this award-winning restaurant overlooking the River Lagan serves creative dishes such as hay-baked beetroot and Skeaghanore duck.

3 James Street South Bar and Grill
MAP L6 ▪ 21 James Street South, Belfast ▪ 028 9560 0700 ▪ £

Renowned for its beef, which is cooked over a charcoal grill, this restaurant has a cool contemporary vibe, and a fantastic drinks menu.

4 Mourne Seafood Bar
MAP L6 ▪ 10 Main St, Dundrum, Newcastle ▪ 028 4375 1377 ▪ £

Large portions of fresh local seafood, including shellfish from the restaurant's own shellfish beds, are on the menu here, as well as steak and chicken dishes.

5 Pier 36
MAP L6 ▪ The Parade, Donaghadee ▪ 028 9188 4466 ▪ £

This award-winning pub-restaurant on the quayside serves great seafood and local game, and bakes its own bread on a range right in the middle of the dining area.

6 The Morning Star
MAP L6 ▪ 17–19 Pottinger's Entry, Belfast ▪ 028 9023 5986 ▪ £

Fine local seafood, meat and poultry dishes feature at this historic 19th-century pub-restaurant.

7 Deanes EIPIC
MAP L6 ▪ 28–40 Howard St, Belfast ▪ 028 9033 1134 ▪ £££

Enjoy modern, innovative cuisine at this Michelin-starred elegant restaurant with flawless service. The tasting menu is a highlight.

Outdoor seating at The Bushmills Inn

8 The Bushmills Inn
MAP K5 ▪ 9 Dunluce Rd, Bushmills ▪ 028 2073 3000 ▪ ££

In the village that produces Ulster's finest whiskey is an atmospheric re-creation of an old coaching inn, with open fires and gas lighting. Try the local beef or fresh salmon.

9 Sooty Olive
MAP K4 ▪ 160–164 Spencer Rd, Derry ▪ 028 7134 6040 ▪ £

Chef-patron Sean Harrigan takes comfort food up a notch at this dapper restaurant-cum-wine bar in Derry's waterside district: go for the bruschetta, burgers and brownies.

10 Crown Liquor Saloon
MAP L6 ▪ 46 Great Victoria St, Belfast ▪ 028 9024 3187 ▪ £

Local favourites are served at this lovely old pub, such as cottage pie and venison and red-wine sausages.

See map on p116

Top 10 Dublin
Streetsmart

A popular pub in the lively Temple
Bar district, Dublin

Getting To and Around Dublin

Arriving by Air

Dublin Airport has two terminals (1 and 2) and is 10 km (6 miles) north of the city centre. From there to the city centre takes 30–40 minutes using the **Airlink** express buses. Two routes run (numbers 747 and 757), with different drop-off points across the city, and tickets cost €6 (or €10 return). Both depart every 10 or 15 minutes from around 5am until 11:30pm. Alternatively, **Aircoach** (route 700) runs 24 hours and costs €7 (€12 return) – the transfer is included with a **Dublin Pass** (see p127). Tickets for both can be bought on board. The no. 16 **Dublin Bus** is a cheaper "local" service to the airport: a single fare costs €2.70. Taxis come in at around €25–30; there is no direct rail link.

Direct flights are available from most major cities in the UK and Continental Europe as well as several hubs in North America. All travellers from Australasia have to fly to Dublin via the UK or Continental Europe.

From the UK, **British Airways**, **Aer Lingus** and low-cost airlines such as **Ryanair** and **Flybe** run regular flights to Dublin and other major Irish cities. They depart from more than 20 UK airports. Aer Lingus, **American Airlines**, **United**, **Delta**, **Air Canada** and **Air Transat** all fly direct to Dublin from cities across the US and Canada; they also fly to Shannon in the south-west of Ireland.

Arriving by Sea

Dublin Port is minutes from the city centre. Dublin Bus no. 53 connects the port with the city's main bus station and city centre once an hour on the half-hour (pay on board), and taxis are readily available, too. **Irish Ferries** runs a cruise and fast ferry service up to six times daily from Holyhead in Wales to Dublin, taking between 1 hour 50 minutes and 3 hours 30 minutes; **Stena Line** operates on the same route four times a day (3 hours 20 minutes). **P&O** offers a car-only service from Liverpool 17 times per week (8 hours).

Irish Ferries also runs services to Rosslare, near Wexford, from Pembroke in Wales; Stena serves Rosslare from Fishguard. And Irish Ferries sails to Rosslare from Roscoff and Cherbourg in France: the crossing takes around 17 hours. **Brittany Ferries** runs a cruise service from Roscoff to Cork, which takes around 14 hours.

Arriving by Road

Eurolines offers a day and night coach service to Dublin from London, Birmingham, Manchester, Leeds and Liverpool via the Holyhead ferry, with journey times of up to 12 hours; also services from Bristol and South Wales using the Pembroke–Rosslare crossing, and from Edinburgh via the Cairnryan–Belfast ferry. Train-and-ferry is quicker, but with bargain air fares available, neither may be an economical alternative.

Getting Around by Train

Ireland's train service is operated by **Irish Rail** (Iarnród Éireann). Some areas such as Donegal are not served by the railway and there are no coastal routes in the south, east or north.

Dublin's suburban commuter network has four main lines: Northern to Dundalk; Western to Longford; South Eastern to Gorey and South Western to Portlaoise. Plus there's the DART, an electric train service covering 31 stations from Malahide and Howth in the north of the city to Greystones in County Wicklow, with a few city centre stops. The last train leaves the city centre at 11:30pm. **Transport for Ireland**'s journey planner is invaluable for planning journeys across train, bus, DART and Luas (see below), and can be downloaded as an app.

Getting Around by Tram and Bus

The **Luas** light railway system consists of two lines, the Red and Green, comprising 54 stations in total.

Dublin Bus runs a comprehensive network, with services running from 6am until 11:30pm. Nitelink Buses operate every 30 minutes from midnight to 4am Friday and Saturday from

St Stephen's Green, Westmoreland Street, College Green, D'Olier Street and O'Connell Street. Green-and-cream bus stops are for the various Hop-on Hop-off tourist buses (see p126).

Beyond the city, the coach network is substantially cheaper than train travel; and **Bus Eireann**'s Open Road pass gives unlimited travel on any 3 days in 6.

Tickets and Travelcards

If you're in Dublin for a few days, the best-value pass is the **Leap Visitor Card**: it straddles bus, Luas, DART and commuter trains. It also works in Waterford, Cork, Limerick and Galway. You can buy your smartcard at one of hundreds of outlets across Dublin, or in advance online, and then top up as you go: there's also an app so you can add credit on the move. Alternatively, you can pay in cash for bus journeys, at stations for rail, or at streetside vending machines for Luas: it is worth considering getting a flexi-ticket which covers 7-day travel.

Getting Around by Taxi

Taxi ranks can be found at the airport, main stations, large hotels and many designated areas around the city. They can also be hailed in the street or called ahead for pick-ups. Fares are metered, with the base rate around €5. There is also the **mytaxi** app which enables you to order a taxi quickly.

Getting Around by Car

Car hire is widespread. At Dublin Airport you'll find all the major car hire companies in the Arrivals Hall at Terminal 1 and also in the multistorey car park at Terminal 2.

There is plenty of parking in the city centre, with electronic signs giving up-to-the-minute availability.

Getting Around by Bicycle

Dublin is extremely bike-friendly, with 75 miles (120 km) of cycle lanes, and there is a **Dublin Bikes** bike-share rental scheme, akin to those run in cities such as London and Paris. Pick up bikes from the 100 or so stations; you will need a credit card to register.

DIRECTORY

ARRIVING BY AIR

Aer Lingus
Ⓦ aerlingus.com

Air Canada
Ⓦ aircanada.com

Aircoach
Ⓦ aircoach.ie

Airlink
Ⓦ dublinbus.ie

Air Transat
Ⓦ airtransat.com

American Airlines
Ⓦ aa.com

British Airways
Ⓦ britishairways.com

Delta
Ⓦ delta.com

Dublin Airport
Ⓦ dublinairport.com

Dublin Bus
Ⓦ dublinbus.ie

Flybe
Ⓦ flybe.com

Ryanair
Ⓦ ryanair.com

United
Ⓦ united.com

ARRIVING BY SEA

Brittany Ferries
Ⓦ brittany-ferries.com

Dublin Port
Ⓦ dublinport.ie

Irish Ferries
Ⓦ irishferries.com

P&O
Ⓦ poferries.com

Stena Line
Ⓦ stenaline.co.uk

ARRIVING BY ROAD

Eurolines
Ⓦ eurolines.com

GETTING AROUND BY TRAIN

Irish Rail
Ⓦ irishrail.ie

Transport for Ireland
Ⓦ transportforireland.ie

GETTING AROUND BY TRAM AND BUS

Bus Eireann
Ⓦ buseireann.ie

Luas
Ⓦ luas.ie

TICKETS AND TRAVEL CARDS

Leap Visitor Card
Ⓦ leapcard.ie

GETTING AROUND BY TAXI

mytaxi
Ⓦ mytaxi.com

GETTING AROUND BY BICYCLE

Dublin Bikes
Ⓦ dublinbikes.ie

Practical Information

Passports and Visas

Visitors from outside the EU need a valid passport to enter Ireland; EU citizens can use national identity cards instead. If you're a citizen of a European Economic Area (EEA) member state and many other countries, including the USA, Australia, Canada and New Zealand, you don't need a visa to visit the Republic or Northern Ireland, and can generally stay for up to three months. Information on which countries need visas can be found on the **Department of Foreign Affairs and Trade** website.

The border crossing between the Republic and Northern Ireland is normally simple, with few formalities, though the UK's exit from the EU may ultimately complicate things. Check with car hire companies that you may take the vehicle across the border. The **Embassy of the United Kingdom** and the **Embassy of the United States** are both located in Dublin, and most other countries also have an embassy or consulate.

Customs Regulations

You don't have to pay duty on goods you bring into Ireland if you bought them in another EU country. However, if you exceed certain quantities, you may be asked by customs officials to show that the goods are for your personal use only. If you're arriving in Ireland from outside the EU, you can bring in certain goods free of duty subject to these limits: 200 cigarettes, 50 cigars or 250g of smoking tobacco; 1 litre of spirits (more than 22%) or 2 litres of fortified wine; 4 litres of wine or 16 litres of beer; 50g of perfume and 250ml of eau de toilette.

Visitors from EU countries should pass through customs using the blue channel after reclaiming their baggage. If you're arriving from outside the EU, you'll need to clear customs. Use the green channel if you have nothing to declare, which means you're not carrying more than the entitled allowances. Use the red channel if you need to declare goods above the duty and tax-free allowance. If you're in any doubt, use the red channel.

For more information on tax and customs consult the **Irish Tax and Customs** website.

Travel Safety Advice

You can get up-to-date travel safety information from the **UK Foreign and Commonwealth Office**, from the **US Department of State** and from the **Australian Department of Foreign Affairs and Trade**.

Travel Insurance

It's advisable to take out an insurance policy that covers cancellation or curtailment of your trip, theft or loss of money and baggage, and healthcare. All EU visitors can claim free medical treatment in Ireland provided they have a European Health Insurance Card (EHIC) from their own country. Cards can be applied for online and are free of charge. To avoid paying for any treatments or prescribed medicines in the event of serious illness, you will need to show your EHIC and some identification, such as a passport. Make sure that the doctor treating you knows that you have an EHIC. Non-EU citizens should check that their insurance covers medical care in Ireland.

Health

In an emergency, dial the **Emergency Services** and ask for the service you require – police, fire, ambulance or coastguard.

Beaumont Hospital, **St James's Hospital** and **St Vincent's University Hospital** all have 24-hour accident and emergency departments in Dublin. **Dublin Dental Hospital** serves emergency dental needs and the **Eye and Ear Royal Victoria Hospital** runs an out-patient surgery every day.

A wide range of medical supplies is available over the counter at Irish pharmacies, although many medicines can only be obtained with a local doctor's prescription. If you have, or are likely to have, special medical needs it's worth bringing your own treatments, clearly labelled, and a letter from your own doctor giving the generic name of any medication you might require. Late-night pharmacies are becoming more common: **Hickey's Late Night Pharmacy** on O'Connell Street in Dublin is open 7 days a week until 10pm.

Personal Security

Like any major city, Dublin has street crime, so make sure you take precautions. It's wise to avoid back-streets or poorly lit areas at night, especially alone. Parts of the Northside can be risky after dark, so stick to main thorough-fares such as O'Connell Street. On the Southside, the area around Dolphin's Barn, beyond Portobello, is notorious for drug-related crime, so avoid that both day and night; the same is true of Summerhill off Gardiner Street on the Northside. Neither area has tourist sights, so you're unlikely to find yourself there unless you're lost.

Elsewhere in Ireland, other than in other large towns, petty crime is seldom a problem. However, it's always best to leave any valuables in the hotel safe when sight-seeing. Beware of pick-pockets, keep handbags fastened, and don't leave items unattended in public places. If you're driving, never leave belongings visible in the car. If you are mugged or attacked, inform the police, known as the **An Garda Siochana** (Gardaí for short): its head-quarters are in Phoenix Park in Dublin, and the city-centre station is on Store Street. To make an insurance claim you must report stolen property to the police immediately. Victims of sexual assault should also contact the **Rape Crisis Centre** on Lower Leeson Street.

The **Irish Tourist Assistance Service (ITAS)** provides practical support to victims of crime and can liaise with embassies, organize money transfers and ticket replacements, cancel credit cards and the like. Main bus and rail stations have lost property offices.

DIRECTORY

PASSPORTS AND VISAS

Department of Foreign Affairs and Trade
W dfa.ie/travel/visas

Embassy of the United Kingdom
29 Merrion Rd, Ballsbridge, Dublin 4
C 01 205 3700

Embassy of the United States
42 Elgin Rd, Ballsbridge, Dublin 4
C 01 668 8777

CUSTOMS REGULATIONS

Irish Tax and Customs
W revenue.ie

TRAVEL SAFETY ADVICE

Australian Department of Foreign Affairs and Trade
W dfat.gov.au
W smartraveller.gov.au

UK Foreign and Commonwealth Office
W gov.uk/foreign-travel-advice

US Department of State
W travel.state.gov

HEALTH

Beaumont Hospital
Beaumont Rd, Dublin 9
C 01 809 3000
W beaumont.ie

Dublin Dental Hospital
Lincoln Place, Dublin 2
C 01 612 7200

Emergency Services
C 999 or 112

Eye and Ear Victoria Hospital
Adelaide Rd, Dublin 2
C 01 664 4600

Hickey's Late Night Pharmacy
55 O'Connell St, Dublin 1
C 01 873 0427
W hickeyspharmacies.ie

St James's Hospital
St James's St, Dublin 8
C 01 410 3000
W stjames.ie

St Vincent's University Hospital
Elm Park, Dublin 4
C 01 277 4000
W stvincents.ie

PERSONAL SECURITY

An Garda Siochana
Phoenix Park, Dublin 8 and 4–6 Store Street, Dublin 1
C 01 666 8000
W garda.ie

Irish Tourist Assistance Service (ITAS)
6–7 Hanover Street East
C 01 890 365700
W itas.ie

Rape Crisis Centre
70 Lower Leeson Street
C 01 800 778888
W drcc.ie

Currency and Banking

The currency in Ireland is the euro, with 100 cents to the euro. Most banks have ATMs (cash machines), which is the fastest way to obtain local currency. Debit and credit cards are widely accepted.

Telephone and Internet

The international dialling code for Ireland is 353, and 353 1 for Dublin. To make foreign calls from Ireland, first dial 00.

Mobile networks in Ireland use European 3G and 4G standards.

Public telephones are mostly card-operated. You can get pre-paid phonecards from some shops and newsagents.

Most lodgings offer internet facilities, and there's free Wi-Fi in many cafés and bars and some public parks and squares.

Postal Services

Postboxes in Ireland are green, and stamps can be bought from newsagents as well as post offices. The **General Post Office** in Dublin's O'Connell Street is open 8:30am–6pm Monday–Saturday.

TV, Radio and Newspapers

The Republic of Ireland has eight national daily papers and six Sunday papers. Quality dailies include the *Irish Times*, the *Irish Independent* and the *Irish Examiner*. Dublin's evening paper is the *Herald*. A good online newspaper is **The Journal**.

Ireland has five national television channels: **RTE 1** and **RTE 2**, **TV3** and **3E**, and **TG4**. There are six national radio stations including an Irish-language service, and many local ones.

Opening Hours

Many museums close on Sunday mornings. Most shops open 9am–6pm Monday–Saturday; Sunday opening is now widespread, but hours are more limited. Banks open 10am–4pm Monday–Friday.

Pubs are open 10:30am–11:30pm Monday–Thursday, 10:30am–12:30am Friday and Saturday, and noon–11pm Sunday.

Time Difference

Ireland is on Greenwich Mean Time, which is 1 hour behind Continental European Time and 5 hours ahead of US Eastern Standard Time. Time shifts 1 hour ahead to Irish Standard Time in summer (roughly April to October).

Electrical appliances

The electrical supply in Ireland is 230v/50Hz. Plugs are of a three-square-pin type.

Weather

Ireland is wet and mild all year round, but generally without extremes. It rarely freezes except in the uplands, while summer can see hot spells.

Travellers with Special Needs

Dublin is becoming more accessible for wheelchair users and people with mobility issues. Most tourist attractions have wheelchair access. Dublin Bus operates some low-floor buses with priority areas for wheelchair users, and most DART stations have elevators or ramps. **Accessible Ireland** has a comprehensive list of hotels, restaurants and transport companies that cater for wheelchair users.

Sources of Information

Tourist information centres in Dublin offer a range of services. **Visit Dublin** on Suffolk Street is the city's main information centre. There is also a branch on Upper O'Connell Street. **Fáilte Ireland**, the Irish Tourist Board, and **Discover Northern Ireland**, the Northern Irish Tourist Board, provide a wealth of information and have centres throughout Ireland. **Discover Ireland** also has a website with listings of information centres, including an office in the Arrivals Hall at Dublin Airport Terminal 2 (6am–7pm daily).

Best of Dublin is an annual magazine with all that's new in the city and is also available online. Other useful websites include **Dublin Town** and **Totally Dublin**.

Trips and Tours

Three companies offer Hop-on, Hop-off bus tours of Dublin. The green buses are run by **Dublin Bus**, the city's public bus operator, the red buses are owned by **City Sightseeing** and the yellow vehicles are operated by **CityScape**.

Several companies offer organized walking tours of Dublin, including **Dublin Free Walking Tour**, with no fixed charge (only donations) for their twice daily tours.

On the **Viking Splash Tour** (see p46) you'll board an ex-World War II landing craft for a lively amphibious jaunt around Dublin's Norse history; while **Sea Safari** is an off-shore adventure from Poolbeg Marina.

The **Dublin Pass** is a sightseeing card offering free entry to more than 25 attractions, plus airport transfer, a Hop-on, Hop-off bus tour and other discounts; it's available for 1, 2, 3 or 5 days.

Shopping

Ireland's iconic products range from Aran sweaters to crystal glass. Seek out ceramics and Celtic jewellery in markets and craft shops: **Kilkenny Shop** and the **Designyard Gallery** are good starting points. **Goodwins** is also a treasure trove of Irish musical instruments.

Where to Eat

Irish stew is the national dish, a boil-up of lamb, spuds and onions. The primacy of the potato still holds – colcannon and champ are both popular variants on traditional mash. But Dublin offers something for every palate, and the food scene has never been more vibrant.

A service charge of 10 to 15 per cent may be added to your bill in hotels and restaurants; otherwise tipping is discretionary.

Where to Stay

Irish Hotels Federation produces the *Be Our Guest* guide, which is available online or in print format. It also earmarks hotels that are wheelchair-friendly.

Keep an eye out for the shamrock symbol. You'll see this above the door of all accommodation that has been approved by Fáilte Ireland or Discover Northern Ireland.

DIRECTORY

POSTAL SERVICES

General Post Office
🆆 anpost.ie

TV, RADIO AND NEWSPAPERS

Herald
🆆 herald.ie

Irish Examiner
🆆 irishexaminer.com

Irish Independent
🆆 independent.ie

Irish Times
🆆 irishtimes.com

The Journal
🆆 thejournal.ie

RTE 1 and RTE 2
🆆 rte.ie

TV3 and 3E
🆆 tv3.ie

TG4
🆆 tg4.ie

TRAVELLERS WITH SPECIAL NEEDS

Accessible Ireland
🆆 accessibleireland.com

TOURIST INFORMATION

Best of Dublin
📞 hotpress.com/bestofdublin

Discover Ireland
Terminal 2, Dublin Airport
🆆 discoverireland.ie

Discover Northern Ireland
🆆 discovernorthernireland.com

Dublin Town
🆆 dublintown.ie

Fáilte Ireland
🆆 failteireland.ie

Totally Dublin
🆆 totallydublin.ie

Visit Dublin
25 Suffolk Street;
14 Upper O'Connell Street
📞 01 890 324 583
🆆 visitdublin.com

TRIPS AND TOURS

City Sightseeing
🆆 citysightseeingdublin.ie

CityScape
🆆 cityscapetours.ie

Dublin Bus
🆆 dublinsightseeing.ie

Dublin Free Walking Tour
🆆 dublinfreewalkingtour.ie

Dublin Pass
🆆 www.dublinpass.com

Sea Safari
🆆 seasafari.ie

Viking Splash Tour
🆆 vikingsplash.com

SHOPPING

Designyard Gallery
🆆 designyard.ie

Goodwins
🆆 goodwinsmusic.ie

Kilkenny Shop
🆆 kilkennyshop.com

WHERE TO STAY

Irish Hotels Federation
📞 00 353 1 497 6459
🆆 ihf.ie

Places to Stay

PRICE CATEGORIES
For a standard, double room per night (with breakfast if included), taxes and extra charges.
....
€ under €100   €€ €100–200   €€€ over €200

Luxury Hotels

The Davenport
MAP G5 ▪ 8–10 Merrion St Lower, Dublin ▪ 01 607 3500 ▪ www.davenport hotel.ie ▪ €€
Housed in a very beautiful Georgian building, The Davenport has traditional, stylish rooms with modern facilities, and a fine restaurant and bar.

The Clarence
MAP D4 ▪ 6–8 Wellington Quay, Dublin ▪ 01 407 0800 ▪ www.theclarence. ie ▪ €€€
This 19th-century building has been spectacularly renovated by the Irish rock band U2, blending wood panelling with cutting-edge modern design. Located in the buzzing Temple Bar area (see pp22–3) and overlooking the Liffey, it is one of the trendiest places to stay in the city.

Dylan
MAP T2 ▪ Eastmoreland Place, Dublin ▪ 01 660 3000 ▪ www.dylan.ie ▪ €€€
A luxurious five-star boutique hotel in Ballsbridge, one of Dublin's most affluent areas, tucked away just off Baggot St and within walking distance of all the city's main attractions. The hotel is superbly stylish and charming, with a relaxing restaurant and impeccable service.

The Fitzwilliam
MAP E5 ▪ St Stephen's Green, Dublin ▪ 01 478 7000 ▪ www.fitzwilliam hotel.com ▪ €€€
Designed by the Conran partnership, this award-winning hotel boasts luxurious rooms and the largest roof garden in Ireland.

The K Club
MAP N5 ▪ Straffan, Co Kildare ▪ 01 601 7200 ▪ www.kclub.ie ▪ Dis. access ▪ €€€
This five-star hotel has two championship golf courses; designed by Arnold Palmer, they are considered to be among the finest in Europe.

The Marker
MAP T2 ▪ Grand Canal Square, Docklands, Dublin ▪ 01 687 5100 ▪ www.themarkerhotel dublin.com ▪ €€€
Dublin's hippest new Docklands address, The Marker makes a bold statement with its check-erboard façade and colour-splashed contemporary interiors. There's a rooftop bar and terrace overlooking the city.

The Merrion
MAP G5 ▪ Upper Merrion St, Dublin ▪ 01 603 0600 ▪ www.merrionhotel.com ▪ €€€
One of Dublin's finest hotels may seem rather unimpressive from the outside, but inside it is the embodiment of Georgian elegance, with ornate plasterwork, antiques, Irish fabrics and marble bathrooms. The modern world hasn't been totally forgotten – there is also a swimming pool, gym and business facilities.

Morrison
MAP D3 ▪ Ormond Quay, Dublin ▪ 01 887 2400 ▪ www. morrisonhotel.ie ▪ €€€
Given that its renovation was carried out by fashion designer and Dublin resident John Rocha, it is unsurprising that behind the Georgian façade of the Morrison hides an interior of supreme style. White walls, Irish carpets and contemporary art are some of its attractions.

The Shelbourne
MAP F6 ▪ 27 St Stephen's Green, Dublin ▪ 01 663 4500 ▪ www.marriott. com ▪ €€€
From the moment you enter the wrought-iron canopied entrance to this beautiful hotel, you will be won over by the grace and charm that have brought loyal customers here since the 19th century.

The Westbury
MAP E5 ▪ Grafton St, Dublin ▪ 01 679 1122 ▪ www.doylecollection. com ▪ €€€
For sheer five-star luxury it's hard to better this classy hotel – the accommodation of choice for politicians and celebrities. It has two fine restaurants and a glamorous cocktail bar and even boasts its own shopping mall.

Three- and Four-Star Hotels

The Croke Park

MAP T2 ■ Jones's Rd, Dublin ■ 01 871 4444 ■ www.doylecollection.com ■ €€

This sophisticated city hotel is right across the road from the legendary Croke Park stadium, the heart of Irish sporting life. It's a real hub on match days. The hotel offers shopping and theatre packages, as well as one that includes a tour of the stadium and the museum.

Grand Hotel

MAP U1 ■ Grove Rd, Malahide ■ 01 845 0000 ■ www.thegrand.ie ■ €€

Many rooms have lovely sea views in this large hotel, located in the charming and lively town of Malahide. There are a variety of restaurants and pubs within walking distance, and the hotel has a heated swimming pool, jacuzzi and gymnasium.

Herbert Park

MAP T2 ■ Ballsbridge, Dublin ■ 01 667 2200 ■ www.herbertparkhotel.ie ■ €€

A modern hotel, with huge windows looking out over lovely parkland. Contemporary Irish art decorates the communal areas throughout, including the lounge and the fine restaurant.

Maldron Hotel Smithfield

MAP B2 ■ Smithfield, Dublin ■ 01 485 0900 ■ www.maldronhotelsmithfield.com ■ €€

This smart hotel has comfortable, modern rooms, some with a balcony overlooking Smithfield Square. It represents really great value in an excellent location. The local pub, The Cobblestone, is a classic, and there's an arthouse cinema next door.

Riu Plaza The Gresham

MAP E2 ■ Upper O'Connell St, Dublin ■ 01 874 6881 ■ www.gresham-hotels-dublin.com ■ €€

Conveniently located on bustling O'Connell Street (see p70), Dublin's oldest hotel, now part of Riu Hotels, sports stunning Waterford crystal chandeliers which add more than a touch of elegance.

Brooks Hotel

MAP E5 ■ Drury St, Dublin ■ 01 670 4000 ■ www.brookshotel.ie ■ €€€

With its dark-wood foyer and bar, Brooks exudes old-world style and elegance. Downstairs, the restaurant sports a more modern decor, reflecting a menu of modern Irish food. The lively pubs and bars of Grafton Street are just minutes away.

Jurys Inn Christchurch

MAP D4 ■ Christchurch Place, Dublin ■ 01 454 0000 ■ www.jurysinns.com ■ €€€

This popular and very comfortable three-star hotel is a great base for exploring the heart of Dublin due to its location opposite Christ Church, with Dame Street, Temple Bar, Trinity College and Grafton Street all just a short stroll away. The rooms are spacious and smart and there is also a hotel restaurant.

The Morgan

MAP E3 ■ Fleet St, Temple Bar, Dublin ■ 01 643 7000 ■ www.themorgan.com ■ €€€

With its minimalist, yet cosy, decor of pale walls, white fabrics and beech-wood furniture, the Morgan encapsulates the contemporary style of the Temple Bar area. In the evenings, it can be noisy on the streets, so it's best to try to get a top-floor room if you possibly can.

The Schoolhouse

MAP T2 ■ Northumberland Rd, Ballsbridge, Dublin ■ 01 667 5014 ■ www.schoolhousehotel.com ■ €€€

This unusual four-star hotel was converted from a 19th-century schoolhouse that saw some action during the Easter Rising (see p39). Many original features have been retained and former classrooms have been converted into a lovely, atmospheric restaurant and bar – fortunately, the modern Irish cuisine is rather better than your average school dinner.

The Spencer Hotel

MAP H3 ■ Excise Walk, IFSC, Dublin ■ 01 433 8800 ■ www.thespencerhotel.com ■ €€€

The Spencer enjoys a perfect central location, a short walk from O'Connell Street and Trinity College. The modern, stylish rooms have floor-to-ceiling windows. You can relax in the heated pool before enjoying a slap-up meal in the American-style steakhouse.

Trinity City Hotel

MAP F4 ■ Pearse St, Dublin ■ 01 648 1000 ■ www.trinitycityhotel. com ■ €€€

This hotel overlooking the walls of Trinity College has paid attention to every detail, combining Art Deco influences with a stylish modern twist. Most striking are its oversized lilac sofas in the foyer, and the great selection of sculptures.

Town House Hotels

Baggot Court

MAP G6 ■ Lower Baggot St, Dublin ■ 01 661 2819 ■ www.baggotcourt.com ■ €

Located a short walk from St Stephen's Green and the shopping hub of the city on Grafton Street, this converted Georgian town house makes an unusual, attractive and affordable place to stay. The price includes a full Irish or Continental breakfast.

Harrington Hall

MAP E6 ■ 70 Harcourt St ■ 01 475 3497 ■ www. harringtonhall.com ■ Dis. access ■ €

A collection of Georgian houses have been combined to provide 28 meticulously decorated rooms. The Irish breakfast is an excellent start to a day of sightseeing, and there is a private car park behind the hotel, a definite bonus in congested Dublin.

Ariel House

MAP T2 ■ 50–54 Lansdowne Rd, Ballsbridge, Dublin ■ 01 668 5512 ■ www. ariel-house.net ■ Dis. access ■ €€

Stately elegance and charming service are on offer at this Victorian

house in a quiet suburb, close to the city centre. The 27 bedrooms are all en suite and tastefully decorated with antique period furniture and pretty fabrics.

Fitzwilliam Townhouse

MAP G6 ■ 41 Upper Fitzwilliam St, Dublin ■ 01 662 5155 ■ www.fitzwill iamtownhouse.com ■ €€

In the heart of Georgian Dublin, near St Stephen's Green, this relaxed and spacious town house, with 13 comfortable en-suite rooms, has lots of charm. It serves a good breakfast, with cheeses and home-made jams on offer.

Hotel St George

MAP E1 ■ 7 Parnell Sq, Dublin ■ 01 874 5611 ■ www.thekeycollection.ie ■ Dis. access ■ €€

The period staircase in this converted Georgian house is one of its most striking features, as well as the glistening crystal chandeliers made from renowned Waterford crystal (see p87). The hotel is conveniently situated for all the literary sights north of the Liffey, such as the Dublin Writers' Museum (see p69).

Pembroke Townhouse

MAP T2 ■ 90 Pembroke Rd, Dublin ■ 01 660 0277 ■ www.pembroketown house.ie ■ Dis. access ■ €€

Exuding classic style, the 48 cosy en-suite bedrooms in this elegant Georgian town house are fully equipped with modern conveniences. Traditional Irish breakfast is offered in the sunny dining room and there is a comfortable lounge.

Roxford Lodge Hotel

MAP T2 ■ 46 Northumberland Rd, Ballsbridge, Dublin ■ 01 668 8572 ■ Dis. access ■ www.roxfordlodge.ie ■ €€

This elegant Victorian town house retains many charming original features. All the rooms are en suite and it is only a short stroll from the city centre.

Trinity Lodge

MAP F5 ■ 12 South Frederick St, Dublin ■ 01 617 0900 ■ www. trinitylodge.com ■ €€

The 26 rooms of this attractive Georgian town house are all elegantly decorated and fully equipped, while the communal rooms are furnished with antiques.

Waterloo Lodge

MAP T2 ■ 23 Waterloo Rd, Ballsbridge, Dublin ■ 01 668 5380 ■ www. waterloolodge.com ■ €€

There are 19 en-suite bedrooms (including several family rooms) in this Georgian town house, which stands in the heart of one of Dublin's most affluent suburbs. The city centre and the Aviva stadium are within walking distance. The lodge also offers free parking, Wi-Fi and a complimentary cooked breakfast.

Eliza Lodge

MAP E3 ■ 24 Wellington Quay, Dublin ■ 01 671 8044 ■ www.thekey collection.ie ■ €€€

This comfortable 18-bedroom guesthouse is located right in the heart of Dublin. Some of the rooms have lovely views of the river and the Temple Bar district is right on the doorstep.

Guesthouses

Donnybrook Hall
MAP T2 ▪ 6 Belmont Ave, Donnybrook, Dublin ▪ 01 269 1633 ▪ www. donnybrookhall.com ▪ €
Situated in the leafy area of Donnybrook, just south of the city, this four-star guesthouse is a family-run concern and is close to many of Dublin's best pubs and restaurants. All of its rooms are en suite and there are several quiet garden rooms and a comfortable sitting room.

Windsor Lodge
MAP N6 ▪ 3 Islington Ave, Sandycove, Co Dublin ▪ 01 284 6952 ▪ www. windsorlodge.ie ▪ €
A haven from the bustle of the city, this striking Victorian home is a short stroll from the DART and Dun Laoghaire with its many shops and restaurants.

Aberdeen Lodge
MAP T2 ▪ 53–55 Park Ave, Ballsbridge, Dublin ▪ 01 283 8155 ▪ www. aberdeen-lodge.com ▪ €€
A friendly, plush boutique hotel on a tree-lined avenue in salubrious Ballsbridge, Aberdeen Lodge serves delicious breakfasts and offers a wonderfully refined setting for a relaxing stay.

Albany House
MAP E6 ▪ 84 Harcourt St, Dublin ▪ 01 475 1092 ▪ www.albanyhouse dublin.com ▪ €€
This elegant, central 18th-century house was once owned by the Earl of Clonmel, and is now a characterful and very comfortable hotel, blending period furnishings with modern amenities.

Dublin Central Inn
MAP F2 ▪ 95–98 Talbot St, Dublin ▪ 01 874 9202 ▪ www.dublincentralinn. com ▪ Dis. access (family rooms) ▪ €€
Excellent value for money, this guesthouse is right in the heart of the city. Bright red sofas and a welcoming fire make up the lounge area, and the bedrooms are stylishly decorated too. The small garden is a bonus in good weather.

Kilronan House
MAP T2 ▪ 70 Adelaide Rd, Dublin ▪ 01 475 5266 ▪ www.kilronanhouse. com ▪ €€
Located in a glorious, leafy part of the city, this lovely, old-fashioned guesthouse is a short walk from St Stephen's Green and the National Concert Hall.

King Sitric
MAP U2 ▪ East Pier, Howth, Co Dublin ▪ 01 832 5235 ▪ www.king sitric.ie ▪ Dis. access ▪ €€
Better known as a fabulous fish restaurant (see p81), King Sitric also offers excellent accommodation, with eight beautiful rooms, all charmingly named after local lighthouses and overlooking the sea. Enjoy the bustle of Dublin by day, then return to this haven of seaside calm.

Waterloo House
MAP T2 ▪ 8–10 Waterloo Rd, Ballsbridge, Dublin ▪ 01 660 1888 ▪ www. waterloohouse.ie ▪ Dis. access ▪ €€
This four-star Georgian guesthouse is run by a family and offers 19 fully equipped bedrooms. It also benefits from a private car park.

Number 31
MAP T2 ▪ 31 Leeson Close, Dublin ▪ 01 676 5011 ▪ www.number31.ie ▪ €€€
This unique hotel, with 21 guest rooms, is comprised of two coach houses (converted by Irish architect Sam Stephenson in 1958), connected by private gardens to a classic Georgian house.

Waterford, Wicklow, Kilkenny and Limerick Hotels

Hunter's Hotel
MAP N5 ▪ Rathnew, Co Wicklow ▪ 0404 40106 ▪ www.hunters.ie ▪ Dis. access ▪ €
Pretty gardens and activities such as golf, tennis, horse riding and fishing are on offer at this old coaching inn. Beaches are nearby and the restaurant takes advantage of the fresh fish for its dishes.

Butler House
MAP P4 ▪ 15–16 Patrick St, Kilkenny ▪ 056 772 2828 ▪ www.butler.ie ▪ €€
Perhaps the most elegant place to stay in Kilkenny, this Georgian town house overlooks the river and the castle. Rooms are spacious, and staircases lead down to the gardens.

Clayton Hotel Limerick
MAP P3 ▪ Steamboat Quay, Limerick ▪ 061 444 100 ▪ www.claytonhotel limerick.com ▪ Dis. access ▪ €€
This 17-storey, landmark hotel in Limerick is right on the waterfront and has great views over the Shannon. Its four-star facilities include a leisure club with swimming pool, sauna and steam room.

For a key to hotel price categories see p128

Hanora's Cottage

MAP Q4 ■ Nire Valley, Ballymacarbry, Co Waterford ■ 052 613 6134 ■ www.hanorascottage. com ■ €€

The beautiful Comeragh Mountains near Hanora's Cottage offer good walking trails, perfect for working up an appetite for the tasty Irish cuisine in the hotel restaurant. Afterwards, you can relax in the hot tub.

Pembroke Kilkenny

MAP P4 ■ 11 Patrick St, Kilkenny ■ 056 778 3500 ■ www.kilkenny pembrokehotel.com ■ €€

Converted from a 1930s racing-car garage, this lovely hotel is right in the heart of Kilkenny. Rooms come with accents of red and super-king beds as standard and there is live music in the bar every Friday and Saturday night.

Rathsallagh House

MAP N5 ■ Dunlavin, Co Wicklow ■ 045 403 112 ■ www.rathsallagh.com ■ Dis. access ■ €€

Once named the Country House of the Year, lovely Rathsallagh House has an 18-hole championship golf course and is set in 530 acres (2 sq km) of rolling landscape with lakes and woodland, located on the west side of the stunning Wicklow Mountains.

Richmond House

MAP Q4 ■ Cappoquin, Co Waterford ■ 058 54278 ■ www.richmondhouse. net ■ €€

This 18th-century Georgian country house offers an award-winning restaurant and stunning grounds. Log fires warm period-feature rooms.

Adare Manor Hotel

MAP P3 ■ Main St, Adare Village, Co Limerick ■ 061 605 200 ■ www.adare manor.com ■ €€€

Situated in one of Ireland's prettiest villages, this 19th-century manor house is a five-star luxury hotel. Once the seat of the Earls of Dunraven, it is now American-owned and has been renovated. Good service is guaranteed.

Mount Juliet Estate

MAP P5 ■ Thomastown, Co Kilkenny ■ 056 777 3000 ■ www.mountjuliet. ie ■ Dis. access ■ €€€

An 18-hole golf course designed by Jack Nicklaus is at the heart of this 1,500-acre (6-sq-km) estate. It hosted the WGC American Express Championship in 2002. The rooms are stunning and it has two award-winning restaurants. There is also a spa and facilities for horse-riding.

Waterford Castle

MAP Q5 ■ The Island, Waterford ■ 051 878 203 ■ www.waterfordcastle resort.com ■ €

One of the unique hotel experiences in the world. The 15th-century castle is set on a sprawling island overlooking the River Suir. Access is by car ferry only and the hotel is luxuriously furnished with antiques and open fireplaces.

Galway and Connemara Hotels

Cashel House

MAP N2 ■ Cashel, Co Galway ■ 095 31001 ■ www.cashel-house-hotel.com ■ €

An oasis of calm in the wilderness of the Atlantic coast, this hotel rests elegantly amid beautiful gardens. Rooms look out onto the gardens or the sea. Antiques and period paintings abound, as do open turf fires. There's a private beach and walks, cycling, horse riding and fishing are available.

Ardagh Hotel

MAP M1 ■ Clifden, Co Galway ■ 095 21384 ■ Open Easter–Oct ■ www. ardaghhotel.com ■ €€

Located in beautiful Ardbear bay, this three-star hotel has 17 rooms, each with a private bathroom. If long walks amid Connemara's coastal scenery don't draw you here, the award-winning restaurant should.

Currarevagh House

MAP N2 ■ Oughterard, Connemara, Co Galway ■ 091 552 312 ■ Open Apr–Nov ■ www. currarevagh.com ■ €€

This country mansion, dating from 1842, is situated right beside Lough Corrib in private woodland. Absorb the splendid isolation of its location by walking in the woods, or take a fishing boat out on the lake before settling down to the popular afternoon tea in the drawing room. The house also has its own tennis courts.

Foyle's Hotel

MAP M1 ■ Main St, Clifden, Connemara, Co Galway ■ 095 21801 ■ Closed Jan ■ www. foyleshotel.com ■ €€

A lovely Victorian-era hotel that offers good, old-fashioned comfort and charm. It has been in the Foyle family for nearly a century, and the smooth service and idyllic location more than make up for some slightly tired furnishings. The attached Marconi restaurant is popular with locals and the breakfasts are famously good.

House Hotel
MAP N3 ■ Spanish Parade, Galway ■ 091 538 900 ■ thehousehotel.ie ■ €€
In the thudding heart of Galway's Latin Quarter, with its buskers and boutiques, this buzzy place fits in perfectly – set in a converted warehouse and home to the city's top cocktail bar as well as some of its crispest bedrooms. The afternoon teas are also superb.

Jurys Inn Galway
MAP N3 ■ Quay St, Galway ■ 091 566 444 ■ www.jurysinns.com ■ Dis. access ■ €€
The Jurys chain offers good value, well-located accommodation. This branch is beside the historic Spanish Arch overlooking Galway Bay.

The Twelve Hotel
MAP N2 ■ Barna Village, Galway ■ 091 597 000 ■ Dis. access ■ www.thetwelvehotel.ie ■ €€
This stylish four-star boutique hotel located near the beach is nestled in the sleepy village of Barna. The luxuriously appointed rooms are individually designed, and there is a pizza kitchen, bakery and a spa on site.

Ashford Castle
MAP M2 ■ Cong, Co Mayo ■ 094 954 6003 ■ www.ashfordcastle.com ■ Dis. access ■ €€€
Facilities include a health club with a steam room

and a sauna at this glorious five-star hotel and resort set in a castle. Activities at the resort include golf, horse riding, falconry, cruising and fishing on Lough Corrib.

Ballynahinch Castle
MAP N2 ■ Ballynahinch, Recess, Connemara, Co Galway ■ 095 31006 ■ www.ballynahinch-castle.com ■ €€€
Once home to the pirate queen Grace O'Malley (see p110), this casually elegant four-star hotel, set in a huge private estate, enjoys a breath-taking location, ringed by the impressive Twelve Bens Mountains. The award-winning restaurant serves fresh, excellent game and fish.

Delphi Lodge
MAP M2 ■ Leenane, Co Galway ■ 095 42222 ■ www.delphilodge.ie ■ €€€
One of Ireland's most famous fishing lodges, the atmosphere here is elegant, with a library, a billiards room and a large drawing room overlooking the lake. Five restored cottages provide further accommodation. The surroundings are home to abundant wildlife, including falcons, badgers and otters. Fly-fishing is offered for salmon.

Cork and Kerry Hotels

The Old Bank House
MAP Q3 ■ 10–11 Pearse St, Kinsale, Co Cork ■ 021 477 4075 ■ www.oldbankhousekinsale.com ■ Dis. access ■ €
Set in two handsome Georgian town houses

facing Kinsale's bustling harbour, this hotel has been voted one of the "Top 100 places to stay in Ireland" every year since 1990. Breakfast, served in the hotel's boutique coffee shop, is excellent.

Aherne's Townhouse
MAP Q4 ■ 163 N Main St, Youghal, Co Cork ■ 024 92424 ■ www.ahernes.net ■ Dis. access ■ €€
This family-run pub is also a hotel-restaurant. The cosy sitting room has an open fireplace and lots of books. Some rooms have balconies.

The Brehon
MAP Q2 ■ Muckross Road, Killarney ■ 064 663 0700 ■ thebrehon.com ■ €€
With a piano plinking quietly in the lobby, a full-service Angsana spa and wide-ranging views of the rugged Killarney countryside, the Brehon is the perfect place to get away from it all. It also wins rave reviews for its terrific food, which is served in both the fine-dining restaurant and the more informal bar area.

Castlewood House
MAP Q1 ■ The Wood, Dingle, Co Kerry ■ 066 915 2788 ■ www.castlewooddingle.com ■ €€
Many rooms boast a stunning view out onto the bay at this luxury guesthouse. Breakfast is hearty and rooms are spacious and stylish, some with jacuzzi tubs. There's a lounge with DVDs and board games. Hosts Helen and Brian are warm and gracious and ensure guests have a comfortable stay.

For a key to hotel price categories see p128

Coolclogher House
MAP Q2 ■ Coolclogher, Killarney, Co Kerry ■ 064 663 5996 ■ www.coolclogherhouse.com ■ €€

Set in extensive parkland, Coolclogher House is within walking distance of Killarney National Park. The large guest rooms have lovely views. The Victorian conservatory here is built around a huge specimen camellia that is over 170 years old.

Muckross Park Hotel
MAP Q2 ■ Muckross Village, Killarney, Co Kerry ■ 064 662 3400 ■ www.muckrosspark.com ■ €€

Located in the heart of Killarney National Park, this plush Victorian hotel has stunning views across the Lough Leane and Muckross Lake. It is home to Cloisters Spa, winner of the Best Destination Spa in Ireland. A true retreat, with staff who go out of their way to make your stay as enjoyable as possible, and sublime food in the Yew Tree restaurant.

Shelburne Lodge
MAP Q2 ■ Killowen, Cork Rd, Kenmare, Co Kerry ■ 064 664 1013 ■ www.shelburnelodge.com ■ €€

Once the home of Lord Shelburne (1737–1805), former prime minister of Great Britain, this beautiful and welcoming guesthouse has roaring log fires and charming, wooden-floored rooms, each furnished with antiques. The house is set in lovely secluded gardens, just a short stroll from the town centre.

Ballymaloe House
MAP Q3 ■ Shanagarry, Midleton, Co Cork ■ 021 465 2531 ■ www.ballymaloe.ie ■ Dis. access ■ €€€

This ivy-covered Georgian guesthouse on a 400-acre (2-sq-km) farm is exceptional. Try your hand at golf or tennis, or splash around in the pool before settling down for a pre-dinner drink in the drawing room. The award-winning restaurant serves wholesome traditional food made with fresh, local ingredients.

The Park Hotel
MAP Q2 ■ Kenmare, Co Kerry ■ 064 664 1200 ■ www.parkkenmare.com ■ Dis. access ■ €€€

Set in a fine 19th-century limestone building, this hotel overlooks stunning gardens and Kenmare Bay. Enjoy the restaurant's mix of classic and inventive cooking, relax in the spa or play a round of golf in the adjacent 18-hole course; salmon fishing and horse riding are also available nearby.

The River Lee
MAP Q3 ■ Western Rd, The Lough, Cork ■ 021 425 2700 ■ www.doylecollection.com ■ €€€

This landmark place makes quite a splash on the Cork riverside, with its glass façade and slick dining terrace. Floor-to-ceiling windows enliven the muted ochres and browns – especially if you opt for a fifth-floor room overlooking the water. There's also an excellent spa, plus an indoor pool and fitness centre.

Sheen Falls Lodge
MAP Q2 ■ Kenmare, Co Kerry ■ 064 664 1600 ■ www.sheenfallslodge.ie ■ Dis. access ■ €€€

This rambling lodge, situated on a dramatic estate above Sheen Falls and Kenmare Bay, is a relaxing retreat set in picturesque surroundings. The renowned restaurant, La Cascade, overlooks a waterfall. There is also a fitness centre, swimming pool and wine cellar.

Northwest and Northern Hotels

The Cuan
MAP L6 ■ The Square, Strangford, Downpatrick ■ 028 4488 1222 ■ www.thecuan.com ■ €

Beside the square in picturesque Strangford, this welcoming guesthouse could style itself as a restaurant-with-rooms, such is the reputation of owner Peter McErlean's cooking. His seafood chowder is near legendary, and you can work off the calories with some walking, cycling or canoeing at nearby Castle Ward.

Bullitt
MAP L6 ■ 40 Church Ln, Belfast ■ 028 9590 0600 ■ www.bullitthotel.com ■ €€

Right in the city centre, the super-hip Bullitt, named after the 1968 Steve McQueen film, offers small but comfortable rooms with bags of personality, including movie-montage art, cool lighting, and "Grub to Go" breakfast bags. There's a sleek courtyard beer garden specializing in craft brews, and a great grill-house restaurant, Taylor & Clay.

Hastings Everglades

MAP K4 ■ Prehen Rd, Co Londonderry ■ 028 7132 1066 ■ www.hastings hotels.com ■ €€

This luxurious hotel is in an ideal location next to the River Foyle and beside the 17th-century walled City of Derry. It's a great base for exploring the town or for venturing further afield into the Sperrin Mountains and County Donegal. Spend your evenings relaxing in the huge lounge bar or dining in the restaurant.

Hilton Park

MAP L5 ■ Clones, Co Monaghan ■ 047 56007 ■ www.hiltonpark.ie ■ €€

The Madden family have been residing in this grand house since 1734, and have been welcoming guests ever since then. The dining room is sumptuous beyond words, and the six bedrooms are superb, with breathtaking views of the woodlands, gardens and lakes.

Radisson Blu Hotel & Spa

MAP L3 ■ Balincar, Rosses Point, Sligo ■ 071 9140008 ■ www.radisson blu.com ■ €€

Offering lovely views of Sligo Bay and the surrounding mountains, this comfortable hotel has 132 rooms with modern decor. It also has a restaurant, bar and leisure club and spa with pool, jacuzzi and sauna.

Rathmullan Country House

MAP K4 ■ Rathmullan, Co Donegal ■ 074 915 8188 ■ www.rathmullan house.com ■ €€

Located on the quiet shores of Donegal, this country-house hotel has award-winning gardens that lead onto a long sandy beach. Rooms are decorated in period style and family rooms and suites are available. There are also an indoor swimming pool, steam room and tennis courts for added luxury.

Tara Hotel

MAP L3 ■ Main St, Killybegs, Co Donegal ■ 074 974 1700 ■ www. tarahotel.ie ■ €€

High and handsome above the harbour in the busy Donegal fishing port of Killybegs, Tara Hotel is known for its smiling staff and hearty breakfasts; ask for a balcony room and watch the trawlers come and go. The spectacular Slieve League cliffs, Europe's highest sea cliffs, are very nearby.

Temple House

MAP M3 ■ Ballymote, Co Sligo ■ 071 918 3329 ■ www.templehouse.ie ■ €€

The Perceval family have owned this lovely Georgian country manor house set in vast grounds since 1665; the current building was refurbished in 1864. Rooms have a traditional atmosphere with log fires and canopied beds. The surrouding area has many archaeological sights and the hotel can advise on walks.

Bushmills Inn

MAP K5 ■ 9 Dunluce Rd, Bushmills, Co Antrim ■ 028 2073 3000 ■ www.bushmillsinn.com ■ Dis. access ■ €€€

Once you check into this old coaching inn and mill house, you may find it difficult to leave. Not only will the open peat fires and gas lights make you want to stay, the nearby Bushmills distillery – the oldest in Northern Ireland – may make you forget how to get home.

Coopershill

MAP L3 ■ Riverstown, Co Sligo ■ 071 916 5108 ■ www.coopershill.com ■ Dis. access ■ €€€

Set on a sprawling estate of farm and woodland, this Georgian mansion is an elegant retreat. Enjoy candlelit dinners served with the family silver, sip drinks by the open log fires and look out for peacocks as you stroll through the beautiful grounds. There are plenty of modern comforts, too.

Whitepark House

MAP K5 ■ 50 Whitepark Rd, Ballintoy, Co Antrim ■ 028 2073 1482 ■ www. whiteparkhouse.com ■ €€€

Owner Bob Isles made headlines in 2003 when he won the AA's "Landlady of the Year" crown, and he still offers impeccable bed-and-breakfast at this atmospheric 18th-century house with a pretty garden behind Whitepark Bay. It makes a marvellous base for the Giant's Causeway and Carrick-a-Rede rope bridge.

For a key to hotel price categories see p128

Index

Acknowledgments

Authors

Polly Phillimore is a freelance writer and editor. She divides her time between Dublin and the West of Ireland.

Award-winning travel writer Andrew Sanger has contributed to a variety of newspapers, magazines and travel websites. He was formerly the editor of *Rail Europe* magazine, and is the author of more than 20 guidebooks, mainly on Ireland, France and Israel.

Additional Contributor
Vinny Crump

Publishing Director Georgina Dee

Publisher Vivien Antwi

Design Director Phil Ormerod

Editorial Sophie Adam, Ankita Awasthi Tröger, Avanika, Michelle Crane, Rachel Fox, Rada Radojicic, Ruth Reisenberger, Sally Schafer

Design Marisa Renzullo, Vinita Venugopal

Cover Design Richard Czapnik

Commissioned Photography Joe Cornish, Rough Guides / Mark Thomas, Alan Williams

Picture Research Susie Peachey, Ellen Root, Lucy Sienkowska

Cartography Casper Morris

DTP Jason Little

Factchecker Therese McKenna

Proofreader Kathryn Glendenning

Indexer Hilary Bird

Illustrator Chris Orr & Associates chrisorr.com

First edition created by Sargasso Media Ltd, London

Guinness Storehouse: 31cr; Enda Cavanagh Photography 6cla, 11cr, 30-1, 31clb.

House of Ireland: 65tr.

Irish Village Markets: 55tr.

iStockphoto.com: Giovanni Caruso 106b; HuyThoai 116c; Wolfgang Schwarz 112cla; stevegeer 87b.

Jam Art Factory: 54clb.

Kealy's Seafood Bar: 115clb.

Kehoe's: 50tl.

Limetree: Barry Murphy Photography 93br.

The Little Kitchen: Killian Broderick 67ca.

This image is reproduced with the kind permission of the National Museum of Ireland: 10cla, 14cla, 14cr, 14bc, 15tl, 15crb.

National Concert Hall: 48br.

National Gallery Ireland: Pierrot (1921) by Juan Gris 10crb; The Liffey Swim (1923) by Jack B. Yeats / © DACS 2017 16cl; Christ in the House of Martha and Mary (c.1628) by Jan Breughel the Younger and Peter Paul Rubens 16-7; Argenteuil Basin with a Single Sailboat (1874) by Claude Monet 17tl; The Cottage Girl (1785) by Thomas Gainsborough 17bc.

Used Courtesy of the OPW, The Office of Public Works: 18cr.

The Olympia Theatre: Dara Munnis 48t.

One Pico: Barry Murphy 67br.

Pichet Restaurant: Andzikdublin.com 53t; Paul McCarthy 2tr, 36-7.

Powerscourt Estate: 75b.

Project Arts Centre: Butterflies and Bones as part of The Casement Project by Project Artist Fearghus O Ó Conchu úir, Photo by Stephen Wright 22bl.

Robert Harding Picture Library: Roy Rainford 106tr; Hugh Rooney 44tl; Peter Zoeller 42bl.

Smock Alley Theatre: 49cl.

SuperStock: imageBROKER 51tl, The Irish Image Collection 61cl.

Taste At Rustic: Ten20photography / Damian Bligh 52cl.

The Bushmills Inn: Kris Dickson 119cr.

The National Maritime Museum of Ireland: 74cra.

The Winding Stair: Dave Sweeney 73cra.

© Trustees of the Chester Beatty Library, Dublin: 20tl, 20bl, 21t, 21bl.

Viking Splash Tours: 46b.

Whelan's Bar: Dara Munnis 51br.

The Wyatt Hotel: 111r.

Cover

Front and spine: Masterfile: R. Ian Lloyd.
Back: Dreamstime.com: Shahid Khan.

Pull Out Map Cover

Masterfile: R. Ian Lloyd.

All other images © Dorling Kindersley For further information see: www.dkimages.com

As a guide to abbreviations in visitor information blocks: **Adm** = admission charge

Penguin
Random
House

First American Edition, 2003
Published in the United States by
DK Publishing, 345 Hudson Street,
New York, New York 10014

Copyright 2003, 2018 © Dorling
Kindersley Limited

A Penguin Random House Company

18 19 20 21 10 9 8 7 6 5 4 3 2 1

**Reprinted with revisions 2005, 2007, 2009,
2011, 2013, 2015, 2018**

Published in Great Britain by Dorling
Kindersley Limited.

A catalog record for this book is available
from the Library of Congress.

ISSN 1479-344X
ISBN 978 1 4654 6781 2

FSC
MIX
Paper from
responsible sources
FSC™ C018179
www.fsc.org

SPECIAL EDITIONS OF DK TRAVEL GUIDES

DK Travel Guides can be purchased in bulk quantities at discounted prices for use in promotions or as premiums. We are also able to offer special editions and personalized jackets, corporate imprints, and excerpts from all of our books, tailored specifically to meet your own needs.

To find out more, please contact:

in the US
specialsales@dk.com

in the UK
travelguides@uk.dk.com

in Canada
specialmarkets@dk.com

in Australia
**penguincorporatesales@
penguinrandomhouse.com.au**

Selected Ireland Index